Software Testing

Interview Questions

You'll Most Likely Be Asked

I0011349

Job Interview Questions Series

www.vibrantpublishers.com

Software Testing Interview Questions
You'll Most Likely Be Asked

ISBN-10: 150537698X
ISBN-13: 9781505376982

Library of Congress Control Number: 2014921802

Vibrant Publishers books are available at special quantity discount for sales promotions, or for use in corporate training programs. For more information please write to **bulkorders@vibrantpublishers.com**

Please email feedback / corrections (technical, grammatical or spelling) to **spellerrors@vibrantpublishers.com**

To access the complete catalogue of Vibrant Publishers, visit
www.vibrantpublishers.com

Table of Contents

This page is intentionally left blank

Software Testing Interview Questions

Review these typical interview questions and think about how you would answer them. Read the answers listed; you will find best possible answers along with strategies and suggestions.

This page is intentionally left blank

SDLC and STLC

1: What is Software and why is it necessary?

Answer:

The term 'software' is related to the web world. In simple terms, it is a solution for a business to systematically manage with production, marketing and sales. The primary goal of creating a software is to make work easy and efficient. Just as the evolution of computer in science has taken next level of living for mankind, software development is becoming a human's friendly tool to get their job done in the expected manner in all possible fields. Designed Software consists of clearly defined instructions that upon execution, performs predetermined tasks. Software is stored in a computer's memory. It is developed by using skill sets of computer like programming languages such as HTML, XHTML, CSS, Java, C, C++ and so on. It also uses databases such as Oracle, SQL server; MS office, Windows Operating, Linux, Apple, UNIX and many more. Networking like WAN and LAN are also used for software to be accessible to many other computers or on the web. Every organization both big and small is on a lookout for best profitable solutions to manage time efficiently for their clientele and hence, software plays an important role in day to day activities. Therefore technology oriented software is a critical survival for every organization.

2: Explain Software development life cycle (SDLC) and its phases.

Answer:

SDLC is also a methodology to build up in a systematic approach. A good software is supported by the architecture. During the process of building software, it goes through several stages. It has 6 phases and they are: Requirement phase, Analysis or planning phase, Design phase, coding and debugging phase, Testing phase, Release and maintenance phase. Based on the requirements, decisions are made to choose a language, database and the appropriate operating system. A proper planning which includes these phases is done by the Team manager or Project manager. A designer prepares the design of the package.

Customers provide information on how and what they want to build, which turn out as Requirements specification document. Based on this information, business is analyzed towards technology judgement, project planning, milestones, and delivery (release) date. This output is called as SRS, System requirement specification. The SRS document is used for coding and writing programs using selected programming language. This outcome is executable software for the next stage with code documentation. The next stage is testing, testers creating test cases as per plan and checking for deviation or defects. If there are errors found, it is sent back to developers to fix the issue. Again, the tester is going to test the fix to sign off. During this phase, documentation is done as part of testing called as test documents. The final stage is Release; the tested software is released to production team or customers in a live environment. Any alterations or defects at this stage is recorded as part of maintenance and goes back to developers and testers. The process of fixing defects and retesting is done until the product is stabilized. Finally, the product is ready for deployment and this is known as SDLC.

3: What kinds of businesses use software and how?
Answer:
Software is used by small, medium or large entrepreneurs. One can come across software in almost every Industry sector like Human resource, Company website, Accounting, Finance, Insurance, Banking, IT sectors, Geology, Geographic information system, Automobiles, Agriculture, Film making, Consumer goods. There are many kinds of software used according to engineering fields like, Application software, System software, SAS software, Embedded software, Tally software, Oracle software, and Computer-aided.
Further, the usage of software can be broadly dissected into:
  a) **Consumer good sectors**- Clothes, Accessories, Shoes, Fashionable products, Photography, and Food.
  b) **Civil services** - software installations in public places like: Malls, Cash counters, CCTV, Hidden cameras, Security

alarms, Medical, Telecommunications, ATMs, Automated traffic signals, Scanners and many more.

c) **Household utilities** - Washing Machines, Air conditions, Grinders, Refrigerators, Computers, Oven, Mobiles, and many more.

d) **Recreation devices** - TV, Toys, and Games.

e) **Computer-aided** - Word processor, Spreadsheets, Mathematical, Servers, Device driver, Operating system, Presentation software, Image making and editing, Vector graphic, Education based software, Multimedia; Internet based software like Email, Messenger, FTP, Video conference, and many more.

4: What is STLC and how is it related to SDLC?

Answer:

STLC is a Software testing life cycle. It co-exists with SDLC. Once SDLC phase with coding is executed, it enters the Testing phase. At this phase 'Software Testing Life Cycle' is evolved. This is a procedure that is generally parallel to the SDLC cycle. There are phases to Software testing just like SDLC. In general, every product needs to be signed off before handing it over to the end party. In technical terms, every product needs a good quality delivery. The process of executing a piece of code (program)or system with the intent of finding errors is a software testing. In other words, evaluation of the software application or program is to ascertain if there is any deviation of actual results with the expected outcome. Its main purpose is to fulfill Correctness, Contents, Security, Reliability, Accuracy, Durability and Completeness. Without a sign off up-on, completion of the STLC process, SDLC is incomplete.

5: With a specific process, how do you differentiate STLC from SDLC?

Answer:

Both STLC and SDLC involve stages or phases and can be differentiated.

SDLC involves the below phases:
Firstly - Initiation of the Project,
Secondly - Requirements and Documentation collections,
Thirdly - designing of product,
Fourthly - Coding,
Fifthly - Unit Testing, Integration Testing, System Testing,
Installation and Acceptance Testing,
Sixthly - Deployment and finally Support and Maintenance is
carried out. Here, the application / product is deployed in a
production environment for real end users,
Seventhly - Maintenance is a post production deployment support
& enhancements.

STLC involves the below phases:
Firstly - Test strategy preparation,
Secondly - Test plan preparation,
Thirdly - Test environment creation,
Fourthly - Test case preparation by writing them in excel format
or word document as per the test plan
Fifths -Test script creation,
Sixthly -Test script execution,
Seventhly -Test results analysis, Bugs reporting through 'tools or
word document or excel file'.

In STLC, retesting the fixed defects or bugs and tests with
regression type is performed. Finally, report is generated based on
the data collected from the end users. Testing team aim is to
check for any gaps to be seen at an early stage by reviewing the
requirements.
SDLC defines what goals to be achieved and how to achieve them;
while STLC carries out support for SDLC to achieve these goals.

6: Who is involved in an SDLC and STLC?
Answer:
As a team, SDLC and STLC have one goal to achieve and are
shared. The project objectives are met by a project manager by

carrying out the work of the project. A project manager roles and responsibilities vary from one company to another. The people who are involved in SDLC and STLC with specific tasks are:
Project manager - Technical Team leader - Developers (Team members)
Delivery head - Test manager - QA lead/Test Lead - Testers (Team members)
Typically, a Business Analyst gathers Requirements. He also works for the UI (user interface) design of the application. The high level & low level designing work of the software is done by Technical architect. Analyzing the requirements from the perspective of design, its architecture & coding, development team begins writing the actual coding.
A Test architect can also be a test lead/manager, who answers the test planning and identifies high level testing points. The test plan is reviewed.
Testing team members review & analyze the requirements. They identify the testing requirements like 'types of testing' required and check for logical functional relationship between various features / modules. Then the Testing team begin to write the detailed test cases. After writing the test cases, test cases have to be reviewed for correctness and coverage of the requirements. Finally, Test Execution is done; defects or bugs are reported by test team members. This stage is called as manual testing. Once the developers accept the defect or bug, they fix it and retesting and regression testing is done by testers accordingly. Deployment is done by developers. Any Maintenance of test cases and relevant documents is done by the test team by updating test plans and test cases for supporting requests and future enhancements of the application.

7: What is a project life cycle?
Answer:
A project life cycle is important to ascertain the essential factors. The path of a project from the beginning to its end represented by different phases is known as the project life cycle.

Every project has beginning period, a middle point, and an ending point. A project can either be successful or unsuccessful. It is a coherent succession of activities to make the project's goals; and accomplish its purpose. Lifecycles differ across industries and business sectors and the methodology chosen for the task. A project typically has the following four main phases: Initiation, planning, implementation, and Evaluation. Every project deliverable produced is reviewed for quality and measured against the acceptance criteria. One of the factors for good project is status reports. It should always draw attention to the expected end point in terms of cost, schedule and quality of deliverables. Once the deliverables are produced, the customer has to accept the final output. And once the customer accepts the final output, the project is ready for sign-off and is deployed. There may be new features development and the above cycle is continued. This is process of different stages is known as a Project Life cycle.

8: Provide details of project life cycle phases.
Answer:
a) **Initiation Phase:**

During the initiation phase, the goal of the project or requirement is identified. This can be an opportunity or a business problem. The cause for the need of the project is documented as a business case with recommended solution options. A possibility study is conducted to explore whether each opportunity addresses the project objective and a solution is finally proposed. Possibility studies like "can we do the project?" and rationalization study such as "should we manage the project?" is discussed.

Once the solution is given and approved, the project is initiated to present the solution. A project manager will be appointed for each project. The participating work groups and the major deliverables are identified. Then, the project team begins to take shape. The project manager approves to begin on the detailed planning phase.

b) **Planning Phase:**

This second phase is the preparation phase. The necessary, planning is done to match the project's objective derivation to the depth of solution of delivering. The team identifies all of the work to be performed. The project's tasks and resource requirements are identified. A strategy for producing them is planned. This is called as 'scope management'. A project plan is produced outlining the tasks, activities, timeframes and dependencies. The project manager finds out cost estimates for the equipment, resource and material costs which are known as a 'project budget'. This is called 'budget management' which is used to discover and organize cost expenditures during project execution.

At this point, anything that might pose a threat to the successful completion of the project is found and is known as 'risk management'. High-threat potential problems are identified. Each high threat potential problem will have an action that is to be taken, either to reduce the likelihood of a problem occurrence or to reduce the impact on the project if it does occur. This is a reasonable time to know all project stakeholders. At last, a quality plan is documented with targets, quality assurance, and control measures along with an acceptance criterion (to meet customer expectations). Thus the project plan is ready to begin.

c) **Execution (Implementation) Phase:**

This is the third phase; the project will commence work as per plan. A project manager spends most of his time at this stage. It is crucial to maintain control of the project. Strict communication is set up during implementation. Project development is consistently watched and suitable tuning is made and recorded if the project deviates from the original plan. Regular team meetings are conducted and progress is communicated and recorded. This data is used to evaluate the performance of the activities and check to see if the results match as per the project plan. Then corrective actions are held as needed. The first course of action is always to bring the project back on course as the original plan. Throughout this step, as per agreed frequency and format, project sponsors and other key stakeholders are informed of project status accordingly. The plan is updated and published on a regular basis.

d) **Evaluation (closure) Phase:**
The final is an evaluation or completion phase. The final deliverables to the customer is released. Project documentation is delivered to the business, supply contracts are stopped, project resources are released and all stakeholders are communicated with the closure of the project.

9: What is the difference between QA and QC and Quality management?

Answer:

QA is Quality Assurance. This is to certify that the whole project life cycle or SDLC processes have a good quality checking system in place. It is process oriented and checks for any faults occurring during the life cycle. It should conform to specified requirements.

QC – QC is Quality control. It is intended to ensure that a manufactured product or performed service meets a defined set of criteria or the requirements of the client or customer. This is product oriented and only detects for errors in product.

QM – QM is Quality management. It is both QA and QC. An organisation with a goal on providing quality services to its customers will always look for better business solutions in the industry for quality and will consistently discover ways to achieve it. QM will implement new technology to accomplish this. It therefore focuses the means to improve with the help of both QA and QC.

QA and QC might also be referred to Verification and Validation.

10: Why is quality important and who is looking for quality?
Answer:
Every business wants quality business or product or services. Providing quality is a significant part of a business market. Industries look for standardizing with quality certifications. Certifications are a trade mark given or attested for any business, product or service that it has passed certain norms, regulations and principles of quality processes as per 'Quality industry standards'. There are certain steps and processes to check for good quality and a good society must adhere to. Otherwise, customers are not satisfied or do not express interest in the job. Every person is a customer who gives profit by making a purchase from the company. They look for quality as a priority to ensure that their money spent is not wasted. The criteria for good quality of industrial products or services, considers many factors like, 'no break down, no cracks, no mall function, durability, reliability, no old or expired food, avoiding unhealthy packing, avoiding cheap materials' and so on. Therefore quality is nothing but, giving approval of businesses that it holds good and liable and dependable commodities. Consumers are looking for trustable goods in this way.

11: What is meaning of prototype in SDLC?
Answer:
A prototype means duplicate. In SDLC, a prototype is an elementary working model of a product or information system. This is generally established to exhibit or built as part of the maturation process. A Prototype Model is a basic version system build. This is a temporary model and not original; which is then tested, and reworked until an acceptable prototype is finally accomplished. The original product or system can then be developed. In this procedure, the client or customer is given the duplicate product design for evaluation. If there are corrections suggested by the client, it is re-shaped to match expectations. Once the client signs off, the original product is produced. This method is used when the client does not provide enough

requirement specifications or has less knowledge of what the product should be for developers. Therefore, prototype model is prepared to show stage by stage developments and mold it with feedbacks. A lot of versions are created during this phase.

12: What is the difference between project, product and application?
Answer:
A Project is the process of accepting a given task or job and completing it for the accepted deadline. There are many kinds of projects involved. This can be developing software, preparing a presentation, creating a model for exhibiting, collecting information for orientation, presenting a seminar, writing thesis and more.

A Product is a substance manufactured for a customer or client to satisfy his need. An item (here, software product) is grown and sold. It is created to perform a task and provide easy, efficient business solutions in the marketplace. Examples are Adobe Photoshop, QTP, Remedy, mobile, thermometer, modem, data card, and any electronic item. Generally products are deployed on the web or connected to wide area network (WAN).

An Application is a software created, generally used within the system to perform some tasks on a daily basis. For instance, developing software for tracking employee work, Status assigning, time taken for daily tasks, QA pass or fail status, and weekly reports. Another example is an HR application with Employee's personal detail information like 'time tracker, check in time, check out time, employee ID, name, address, health details, Team and designation'. The application is deployed for local area network (LAN) and is an internal purpose. Apart from this, an application can be used to help with many features within the mobile and computers itself.

13: What are the objectives of a good software testing?
Answer:
There can be many objectives of testing a software. They are,

a) To determine if the product is meeting the client business requirements
b) To determine if the product conforms to the functional requirement specifications
c) Review of requirements must be done.
d) To determine user acceptability
e) Deliberate finding of errors or bugs or defects
f) To make sure that the system is ready to use
g) To make sure that a system performs as required
h) To prepare a good Test plan and Test case coverage with high probability of detecting defects
i) To check for proper documentations
j) To have good bug life cycle system in place
k) With a minimum amount of time and effort, test cases should show errors of each module
l) Testing should ensure that the software is ready for use
m) To have good checking measures for the systems' condition under extreme stress.
n) Conduct peer review of test plans
o) Identify hazards and have strategies ready

14: What is the goal of a tester and how to attain it?
Answer:
There are many ways to conceive how a testing should be performed by an examiner. The main goal of the team is to win. The examiner should identify faults. There are numerous aspects to be considered while doing the test.

a) To test the product or application from the end user standpoint
b) To test from the developer point of view
c) To test from the layman point of view
d) To test from the production team point of view
e) To examine the application as per the Test plan
f) To test from the Design point of view
g) To test from the Requirement point of view
h) To test from the point of Business specifications

i)   To test as per the new technology implementation
j)   To test as per the Testing standards
k)   To write good test cases and traverse the whole
     requirement
l)   To check as per the Test Cases and Test Strategy
m)   To give inputs to the system and assess the outputs.
n)   To interact with the product or system to the deepest
     layer.

15: What is the cause of software failure?
Answer:
There are many factors that indicate a software failure. The
package is a failure, if it shows a defect to the client after
deployment/delivery. The factors for failure can be any of the
below,

a)   Preparing wrong requirement and is not as per the
     customer needs
b)   Requirements are missing
c)   Unrealistic requirement implementation
d)   Wrong designing of the product or application
e)   Coding errors, coding is not properly managed.
f)   Implementation of design is improper
g)   Software functionality does not show as per the client
     needs.
h)   If the testing levels are not performed well
i)   Improper configuration management
j)   If there are some missing steps in testing methods
k)   If testing types are not followed correctly
l)   If test case coverage does not cover the requirement
     specifications
m)   Environment setup fault
n)   If stress testing does not take care
o)   Failure in proper system maintenance
p)   When the software system is old and user tries to stress
     with new inputs which was not part of the final release.

This page is intentionally left blank

Testing and Methods of Testing

16: What is Testing or Software testing?

Answer:

Testing is done during the process of development to access the quality of product. In other words, software testing is a V2 process, which is Verification and Validation process. At the beginning of the testing phase, there should be no errors and testing should meet the requirements. This process of checking error free process at the beginning of a development is called as verification. During the end phase, product should meet the end client requirement. This is called validation. A product or application, both needs testing. It is measuring the outcome or benefits as per the client. It is important that the product is accepted by the stakeholders, production people and target audience. At the end, it should satisfy the customer. Testing can be successful or meaningful, when it is done with the purpose of obtaining errors. The eye for capturing a mistake is the characteristic of testing. An examiner possesses this character and the process is called as Software testing.

17: What is Test Control?

Answer:

Control Test is to ensure that there is control on an unexpected situation with respect to test plans and timelines. This is to ensure that the alternative actions are taken to achieve the best outcome of testing. In other words, it is management of tasks through the testing process in parallel with the software development process without disturbance in the organization needs and project demands. Several unexpected situations can arise with respect to team member absence or team member leaving the company, or client's sudden requirement changes with less testing time. Example: A software piece has come to test at a later stage than the planned stage from the development phase, but the release date cannot be extended due to market demand or client delivery. This is the point when test control emerges to re-prioritize testing plan to fit what is available on that front for testing. Another instance: During performance testing, when the production team extends their working hours due to unexpected huge traffic, they automatically occupy Testing team hours. This needs Test Control, testing is thus carried out by pushing performance testing schedule to the weekends, while the production team is not working on the application during weekends.

18: What is Test Estimation and how is it done?
Answer:
Test Estimation: Estimation is basically judgement and first thing that comes to mind about Test Estimation is evaluating cost, resources and timelines. It is an important role for a project manager to practice evaluation of a project and ensure building good reputation with the customer. Building a promising estimation will build good customer relation. Failing of an estimation phase, will result in missing the project deadlines and hitting ROI, and lose customer's trust. Any awful estimation may also result in poor work distribution and responsibilities among the team members. It is not an easy task, and various factors need to be considered to build estimation. Firstly, prior experience within the team for a team member and a leader will help note the challenges in the process of delivering a product. Working on various projects as 'project lead' will help prepare precise estimation for testing cycle. Test estimations should always be realistic. Some other ways to achieve this is:
   a) Ensuring availability of resources during this period
   b) Knowing our team well
   c) Taking buffer time if needed
   d) Performing parallel testing if possible
   e) Revisiting the estimations before final commitment in initial stages
   f) Performing Load Test
   g) Checking the Scope of Project
   h) Track the Bug Life Cycle: Make sure all the bugs are resolved as planned on time.

19: What are the different types of Test Estimation?

Answer:

The different types of Test Estimation are:

Ad-hoc Method - In this method, the testing efforts are based on uncertain time frame. The timeline is set by a manager or by client with less knowledge or by marketing personnel with no experience.

Analogy and Experts Based – Test estimation in this method is done by collecting Metrics from Previous tests; by applying knowledge gained by a similar application tested in previous project; by asking subject matter experts who know the application testing very well and taking notes of it.

Work Breakdown Structure – In this method, test project is broken into small pieces as Modules. Modules are broken into sub modules. Sub modules are divided into Functionalities. Functionalities are further divided into sub functionalities. Reviewing is done for all the requirements to make sure they are added in the Work Breakdown Structure. Estimation is done based on time taken for these tasks (each breakdown) by counting the number of tasks the team needs to complete.

Delphi Technique – Is similar to the above WBS. Here functionalities and each task are distributed to each team member. Then the team member in turn yields an approximation of how many hours needed to finish the task. This technique gives good confidence in the estimation because of the team member analysis and commitment. This technique can also be merged with other techniques for a better estimation.

Percentage Distribution – All the phases of SDLC are divided into parts and 100 percent efforts are assigned to them. The divisions are: Project management: 10%, Requirements: 10%, Design: 15%, Coding: 25%, Test (all test phases): 25%, Documentation: 10%, Installation and training: 5%. This allotment of percentage may vary from project to project or organizations.

Testing Point Analysis - Under Test Point analysis, Estimation is based on the following needs to be carried out:

    a)   Static Test Points

b) Dynamic Test Points
c) Productivity Factor
d) Test Control Factor
e) Environmental Factor
f) Preliminary Test Hours
g) Total Test Hours

20: What is the difference between a Developer and a Tester?
Answer:

Developers and/or Designers approach software with an optimised mind set. Their hypothesis is that the changes made by them or solution provided by them are the true problem remedies. Therefore, it is just assumed based thinking. Developers usually omit primary doubts in specification documents in order to complete the project or fail to identify them. These ambiguities are hidden and developers build codes. They are always working on a deadline and it is by nature to overlook the minor details. As a developer, his primary task is to build the software or product with meeting the deliverable timelines. They cannot and do not investigate the details. A developer's assumption lead to a bug as viewed from the end-user needs or business requirement specifications.

This is why a Tester is required to look for mistakes as his job. The mindset of a tester is always asking questions like, Why? How? When? What? A Tester digs into the product layer by layer. In other words, he does not go by the face value of the merchandise and is constantly questioning every occurrence. This doubtful nature of a Tester leads to finding the mistakes. On another note, development team can also be testers; only when they stop coding and check their codes for mistakes like in a Unit Test. Also other tests can be performed by developers, by adopting the state of mind similar to a Tester. This reduces cost of the project and offers better quality in the initial phases of SDLC.

21: What are Testing methods? Describe their characteristics.
Answer:
There are basically two methods of testing, Static testing and Dynamic testing.
Static testing: In this testing, the actual Software is refrained from testing. It mainly checks for the common sense of the code, document or algorithm and is not a detailed test. It verifies for code or called as code review and manually reviews requirement and specification documents. The intention of checking is towards completeness. Both Testers and developers perform this test. The types of Static Testing are Code Analysis, Inspections, Reviews, and Walkthrough. Static testing can be done with other software tools; and is the automation of static testing. Static testing involves verification process.
Dynamic Testing: This is a detailed test. Dynamic testing is usually performed by Testers. A given set of test cases is used to execute programmed code and this is known as dynamic testing. This testing can be done even before writing of the code is completed. These are referred to modules and discrete functions. In the dynamic testing, the software is compiled and run. It also calls for feeding input values to the software and inspecting the output as per the test cases. These Input and output values are taken from test cases and executed. This testing can be done manually or with the aid of an automated tool. There are testing techniques and they are done by using stubs, drivers or executed from a debugger environment. Dynamic testing involves validation process.

22: What is a White box testing stage?
Answer:
This is one of the traditional methods of testing.
White box testing involves assigning tasks to the team during the SDLC phase. This is one of the first phase or stage. It is known with other terminologies and they are 'Clear box testing, Transparent box testing, Structural testing and Glass box testing'. It tests internal construction or behavior of a program. In white

box testing, knowledge of programming skills, and knowledge on an internal outlook of the system, is needed to design test cases. This process involves picking up inputs to run through paths into the code and shaping the relevant outputs. Developers test the code by running it using a tool. This involves Unit testing level. Sometimes it is also involved at integration and system levels of the software testing process. Testing paths within a unit is Unit testing. Testing paths between units is Integration testing. Testing paths between sub systems is a system level testing. This method of test design can recover many errors. Though, it may fail to detect, if there is a missing requirement or yet to be implemented feature. Usually developers are involved in white box testing, but are not restricted for Testers to test. Thus it is testing the internal mechanism which checks for 'how a system should work'.

23: What is a Black box testing stage?
Answer:
This is second type of traditional methods of testing.
Black box testing is also known as Functional and /or Behavioral testing. There are functional requirements and test cases are written based on this specification. This phase is the second stage of SDLC process. It involves checking of the system or product or software according to the Functional requirement specification. It determines if the software does what it is supposed to serve. This method does not touch on internal code checking. That means exploring functionality without internal implementation knowledge. The testing name is such because it treats the software as a black box, meaning unknown system. Usually, the Tester is involved in black box testing and not a developer. A tester does not know how software performs but knows only what the software is supposed to react. Black box testing methods are many: boundary value analysis, equivalence partitioning, state transition tables, all pairs testing, fuzz testing, decision table testing, use case testing, model based testing, specification based testing and exploratory testing.

24: What is a Grey box testing?
Answer:

Grey box testing evolved from combination of White box testing and Black box testing. It seeks for knowledge of algorithms and internal data structures for designing test, to help execute these tests at the black box level testing or user. In this method, there is no need for a tester to have complete access to the software's source code. There is no specific input value or output value while testing Grey box unlike black box test cases. This is particularly true when performing Integration testing. Grey box is good testing choice in-between two modules of code which are written by two different developers and only have interfaces exposed for test. Grey box testing has reverse trade to resolve, situations like boundary value analysis or error messages. A Grey box testing is done for a back end data in a database or a log file for updating or changing data that a production user normally will not be able to make any change.

In this method, a tester can watch the behavior of the product being tested after certain actions in isolation set up environment like, executing SQL statements or queries to ensure that the changes are reflected.

25: What is a requirement testing?
Answer:

Requirements testing: Under this testing, for every requirement, a set of tests are derived. It is part of product or process development. This is a document that outlines physical and functional needs of a product or system and is required to perform accordingly. It may contain design, service, material, process and more. Requirements show what fundamentals and functions are necessary for the particular project.

This is a major input in developing a product as per the customer need. It has statements that identify all necessary attributes, characteristic, quality or capability of an organization.

Requirements are an important input into the verification process. Tests should trace back specific or most defects in a system like missing, incomplete, wrong, or vague requirements. Thus, testing these requirements involves the stakeholders like Developers, Testers, Project manager, Sales head. There will be a review of the document and checking for any missing or changed needs of the client and making necessary timely updates. On the contrary the requirement should be checked for unambiguous, correctness, logically consistent, and complete details. This ensures better documentation and requirement testing.

26: What are reviews, inspections, peer review or walkthroughs?
Answer:
A **review** is examining and in testing, it is less formal. It involves stakeholders in a meeting with an agenda and moderator and goal set. Simple content written mistakes are corrected and all stakeholders read the material before the meeting and actively take part. Other business queries, doubts and concerns related to the requirement are discussed based on the roles assigned at the meeting. The Moderator, Reviewers, Scribe / Recorder, Author are all the important participants of reviews. Modifying the requirements based on several meetings is the process of reviews. There are many activities to and fro taking place before the actual process should begin or is decided to begin. The review is then closed after every stakeholder has agreed on the purpose of meeting.
An **inspection** is part of the review and is led by a trained moderator using Entry and Exit criteria.
A **walk-through** is similar to review and is led by an Author.
A **peer review** is reviewing of requirements or documents or test cases by a team member (colleague) with the same designation. All the above methods are based on a different organizational decision.

27: What are the techniques used in white box testing?
Answer:
White box testing is also known as static testing. Apart from this, below are few testing techniques in white box.

API testing – An API is an application programming interface, testing of the application is of two types and they are public and private APIs. It is a collection of programming functions and procedures, called as API calls which can be executed by other software applications. Under testing, a test harness is constructed to replicate the user of API by end user applications.

Code coverage – It is the degree to which a source code or a program is tested by a test suite. In other words, it is to discover how much of the code has been implemented by running the tests.

Fault injection methods –This is a method for introducing faults intentionally to gauge the efficiency of testing strategies. Faulty inputs are injected to test code paths like, error handling, protocols, and APIs and command line parameters and so on. It is greatly considered during stress testing, robust testing.

28: Does testing start early in SDLC?
Answer:
An effective SDLC is observed when early mistakes are found and rectified. Therefore, adopting early testing is a good SDLC method. The major factor for testing to start early is because finding defects later in SDLC are expensive to fix, than the defects identified in early stage. This statement is especially true if there is, not much time for a product development or less time for the testing phase. That is if the project timing is flexible, then testing can start after development or at any stage of development. At this point, model selection is executed accordingly. Generally, fixing a bug at a later stage is costlier and is stressful for both developers and testers nearing to the release and deployment time. Some other key factors to be considered for an early life cycle are:

a) Testing project's requirements at an early stage.
b) Completion of writing test cases early to help rewrite or update test case if requirements change.
c) Early test environment preparation will prevent delays. Consequently, there will be a time good enough to deal with unknown dangers.

29: Do requirements change continuously and how is it done?
Answer:

In Software Application Development, requirements may or may not change. Most of the web based developments usually have changes in requirements or installed applications have requirement changes as the new technologies are getting introduced. It is important that the changes are communicated well in advance and enough time is given to testing the application without having problems for testing at all.

In a situation where there is not much time for testing, there should be an alternate test strategy and test plan prepared in advance.

a)   Rapid prototyping should be opted for best results. Customers will feel sure of their requirements and minimize on any changes.

b)   Automated tests should be created thoughtfully such that any change in requirements will not affect the automated tests and reduce wastage of time.

c)   If changes are made to requirements, prepare a risk analysis first to minimize the effort of regression testing later.

d)   Developers can make code changes easily if the code is well documented and well annotated.

e)   It is good practice to think about probable changes in the requirements in the initial stages of projects.

f)   If specific requirement is changed, preparing for 'requirements traceability matrix' will help to trace specific test case updates.

30: Does the software have a risk based testing, how is it resolved?
Answer:

Risk based testing involves software testing based on priority with features, importance, functions and potential failures. Any project is first identified with risks. Then this risk is analyzed with potential cost expenditure. Tasks usually have many constraints like resources, quality requirement with respect to organization standards, and time. This is when risk based testing is best suited. In implementing new projects, lack of knowledge, technology, and lack of experience is high risk factors involved. Some steps to be considered are,

a) Have a full understanding of the advantages and disadvantages for this kind of testing.
b) Identifying how and when to use Risk Based Testing.
c) To understand steps to implement an appropriate application.
d) To design risk free project by applying best practices in risk management analysis and achieving best results that balances risks related to features, quality, schedule and budget.
e) Precise understanding of requirements specification, design documents and other documents.

31: Define Data flow analysis testing technique.
Answer:
Data flow testing involves developing test cases to understand the data flow within the coding. The analysis can be done by simple review of the source code or it can be done by executing the actual program. Basically, information is collected on a set of values used for calculating in a program or code. Variables are assigned with values with a certain association and this investigation of how the program is executed is known as Data Flow analysis. In simple understanding it is to identify the path, when a program code is executed, from initialization of a variable, to assigning a value and performing calculations (like conditional statements) and assigning resulting value to another variable. These variables may be used as predicate expressions. Compilers can be used for collecting information of variables. In this method of testing, a Data flow graph is created to check the values, and path is identified and predicate expressions are created.

Levels of Testing

32: What is the Myth in testing?

Answer:

In a SDLC, there are many myths related to testing. Testing is an essential part of the SDLC.

A testing is expensive – It can only be expensive if it is not implemented at early stages.

Testing is time consuming – Planned life cycle never consumes time and whatever time utilized, is a productive activity.

Tested software is always Bug free – This is strong myth. A software system is always communicating and thus even with 100% defects rectified; a software need cannot be bug free.

Testing is always complete – Though all paths are tested, there may be scenarios where testing is executed done after deployment.

Missing defects are due to testers – Costs, Requirement changing constraints and Time are the main culprits for less scope in testing. Defects may arise due to these factors and a good test strategy ensures this myth of testing as false.

Automation can save time always - Automation can only save time when thorough manual testing is done and the system is stable with no changes in requirements.

Only testers are responsible for quality product – Testers are only responsible for identifying issues, but not fixing these issues. Developing finished good product is the job and the responsibility of stakeholders under that project management before committing for delivery.

Without fully developed product, testing cannot start – Testing can still start with review for requirements and developing test plans and test cases.

Testers' task is only to find bugs – If testers only find bugs, then any one can test. Testers are experienced and have domain knowledge. Any product without requirements and specifications can still be tested though experience. The Testers know the need, and overall structure of the software being developed.

Anyone can test – As said above, testing needs thinking out of the box and thinking alternatives to crash a system. Testing approach needs acting in every kind of a user in that field.

33: Can a Fresher without knowledge, perform manual software testing? How?
Answer:
Usually, a fresher is assumed to have knowledge about Software Testing before beginning of a real client work. They will have this knowledge either from the Educational Qualification or from Private Institutions. It is unusual that a fresher without knowledge is found working as a Tester. But as a rare case, for any internal transitions or due to other business project variation a fresh team member is created and installed for a Testing project. Thus the fresher needs specific training. This candidate may have knowledge or have 0% knowledge of testing and the latter become good Testers with the help of effective training process within the organization. There will be a software testing trainer or a Senior Quality Tester to train the team member. There will be training documents like User manuals, guides and documents related to the learning. A fresher gets help from any 'software testing concepts' manuals available within the company during the training period of three months. This process of training usually takes three months and is an investment in the company. A team member may also enroll in several online courses or attend seminar to gain latest testing knowledge. Once the training is done, to get a better understanding and to perform well with a real work project, it is good to have a Testing certification.

34: What are levels of testing and their use?
Answer:
There are 4 standard types of testing and are the major ways of testing as per the V model testing. They are listed as below:
   a) **Unit or Component Testing:**
      This testing is done by Developers as the first stage in the testing life cycle. After a requirement analysis is done, designing is made, Programming is written, developers perform Unit testing to check if there are any defects in

each piece of code. In this testing, executing a piece of code to check for errors is known as Unit testing. Developers may also test this with the help of a testing tool. This code can be written in languages like .Net, C, C++ or Java.

b) Integration Testing:

This is the following stage of Unit testing. In this stage, one or more individual pieces of codes are combined together to form a component. This interface testing is Integration testing where smaller codes are built in units and Units are combined to form components (big coded programs), and components are combined into modules. To check the possibility of errors at each step of combining codes is integration testing. In this case, performance, functional, and requirement purposes are checked. An Integration testing has three approaches of testing, they are: Big-bang, Top down, Bottom up and Umbrella approaches.

c) System Testing:

The Third stage of testing is System testing. While Unit and Integration testing is involved in integral code testing, system testing is external testing related to requirement specification documents. This testing is done from the client and end user's perspective.

After the completion of Integration testing, system testing is begun to check for completeness of integrated applications along with external peripherals (like keyboard, mouse, network, Database, FTP and more) to understand how the components behave. System testing falls under the black box category. This is also called as End to End scenario testing.

d) Acceptance Testing:

The final level of testing is Acceptance testing. The approach of testing is to satisfy the end users or client requirement specification. The production team and the client or end user will be testing the final product. A parallel live environment is set up to feel the real time scenario. No defects should be found at this stage as the criteria of testing. This is to check if the product is ready for final deployment. A beta stage testing is carried on at this level.

35: Elaborate on types of Integration testing.
Answer:
Big Bang approach – Individual modules are combined together to make a complete software and then tested. This approach is time consuming; and since integration testing is done after all the components are combined, defects are found at a later stage.
Top down approach – In this approach, all high level modules/units are integrated and tested first. Later lower level (sub modules) units are examined step by step from top to bottom. The high level logic and data flow are tested at an early stage and a result easily finds a missing branch link. This approach uses Stubs.
Bottom up approach – This approach uses Drivers. It involves all low level units' integrated and tested first. Later high level codes/units/components and data flow are tested step by step from bottom to top. As a result bugs are found more easily.
Umbrella or Sandwich approach – The combination of top down and bottom up approaches is known as Sandwich approach. This involves testing both control flow paths and functional data. This approach may not need Stubs and Drivers.

36: What are the advantages of unit testing?
Answer:
The advantages of unit testing are:
   a) **It is quick**: It takes less than a second to run a unit test.
   b) **It is repeatable**: The tests can be re-run many times unless requirements are changed.
   c) **No memory required**: It does not depend on anything in memory (ex: databases, file system, network). No memory usage.

d) **It is consistent**: Running the code every time, gives the same result
e) **Easy updating: Codes can be changed easily.**
f) **Early defects**: Defects are found at an early stage and can be fixed immediately without giving room to fix them at the final testing level.
g) **Cost saving**: Since the defects are found early and fixed, the cost of the project is reduced.
h) **Good ROI**: Due to less time on the final stages of software testing and repeated code execution, good ROI (Return on investment) is generated.
i) **Automation**: Stable codes can be automated for Automation testing.
j) **Design improvement**: It can improve designing with test driven development.
k) **Bringing Confidence**: It can boost confidence to developers.

37: What are different types of system testing?
Answer:
There are many types of System Testing. The major system testing types are:

a) **Load Testing** – The software is tested under real life loads (volumes) to check its performance.
b) **Usability Testing** – The software is tested in view of a user for, flexible controls, easy use of the application, understandable features and the system's ability to meet its objectives.
c) **Recovery Testing** – The software is tested for reliability and trustworthiness. It is also to check if the system can recover from potential crashes.
d) **Regression Testing** – The whole software is tested for other possible new rise of defects after a certain bug is fixed and re-tested. This is also to ensure detection of old bugs recurrences over time due to additional software modules.

e) **Functional Testing** – This testing involves checking any missing functions as part of standardizations. Testers think of applying functionalities where ever necessary for a complete meaningful product.

f) **Hardware Testing** – The software is tested for defects when it is connected to other hardware products or applications. It is basically testing interactions between the hardware and software.

g) **Migration Testing** – The software is tested for defects when a system is moved from the old infrastructure to new infrastructure.

38: How is system testing carried out?

Answer:

Every level of testing has Entry and Exit Criteria and this should be checked.

Entry Criteria are:

a) Unit testing stage should be completed.

b) Modules should be fully Integrated and tested.

c) Software development should be completed as per specification document.

d) Testing environment should be setup for system testing, which is known as staging environment.

Exit Criteria should be:

a) Preparing for Test Plan – Test planning like Test strategy, entry and exit criteria and more should be considered.

b) Creation of Test Cases - Test case needs to ensure coverage of all User Interface requirements, functional, technical, and non-functional types.

c) Creation of input data which is used for System testing

d) Preparing of automated test case execution scripts by identifying stable test cases.

e) Execution of test case & updating test cases if any test management tool is used.

f) Preparing for Bug life cycle & performing Regression testing.

g) Considering repetition of the testing life cycle as required.

39: List out differences between Unit and Integration Testing.
Answer:

Unit Testing	Integration Testing
Results are dependant only on coding language	Results depend on both Unit testing and external systems
It is easy to write a code and verify	Integration testing set up might be complicated
Testing is done in isolation for each class/unit	Testing is done for one or more components together
Only the implementation of the code is verified in this testing	Testing done here, verifies functioning of individual components along with their interface behaviour when combined together.
All dependencies may or may not be mocked	Mocking is used only for unrelated component
Testing uses only JUnit or TestNG with a mocking frame work if needed	An integration test can use the real database connection. Also, it may use integration testing frameworks.
If a test case execution fails, then it is always a failure unless the business spec has not changed.	If test execution fails, it can either be code error or the set up environment has changed.
Mostly Developers perform Unit Testing	Testing can be performed by Developers, Testers and is useful for the Help Desk

40: What is debugging?
Answer:
Debugging is the process of locating and fixing bugs or errors in computer program code. It can also bypass bugs. Debugging is done by starting with a program or hardware device problem,

isolating the source code of the problem, and then fixing it. Every new software or hardware development process requires debugging; whether it is an enterprise, a personal application program or a commercial product. Debugging is done as the result of the unit testing or Integration testing (when parts are combined together) and/or System testing (when the product is used with other peripherals). Debugging is also done as a result of client beta stage testing or acceptance testing (when end users try the software in a real world situation). Hardware devices contain thousands of lines of code; almost any new product is likely to contain a few bugs. Debugging is usually performed by Developers at the unit test level. Testers may also perform at other levels of testing.

41: How can mistakes be classified in testing?
Answer:
Testing life cycle uses tags for a mistake or error at different stages and is commonly called in different terms. They are:

a) **Mistake** – When a requirement specification contains wrongly typed in sentences, improper grammar, or spelling errors, then it is known as a Mistake. A human interference with the system and their error performance is known as a Mistake.

b) **Anomaly** – Anomaly is similar to a defect. It is a result that is different from the expected result. This is referred to as a tester's opinion or behavior resulting from a document.

c) **Failure** – When a final product does not meet end user's business requirements, then it is called a Failure product.

d) **Exception** –There are certain outstanding conditions when the system does not handle properly and leads to system crash. When things appear in a system, which is not a part of normal operation is known as Exception.

e) **Error** – When a code does not give an exact result is known as an error.

f) **Fault** – When a computer program results with an incorrect data definition or step or process, the program behaves in an unanticipated manner. This is called as a fault.

g) **Crash** – A product or system does not respond to any user actions further as a result of previous action. It completely stops from responding and needs immediate developer attention to fix. This state is known as system crash.

h) **Defect** – When an actual output result does not meet with expected input result as per the test cases tested by a Tester is known as a Defect. In other terms, an error found by a Tester is a Defect.

i) **Bug** – It is a coding defect. A potential defect accepted by the development team is called as a Bug.

j) **Malfunction** – A functional behavior other than it is intended to be known as a malfunction.

k) **Side Effect** – An error causing another error is called as Side effect.

l) **Flaw** – A flaw is an intermediate level for a Bug. It is a defect hidden in a software design and gets implemented in a code.

Types of Testing

42: What are the different types of testing?

Answer:

There are numerous testing types. They are sometimes simply called by different names. These testing types have evolved as per the product types and its service levels and organization's standards.

a)   A/B testing
b)   Alpha testing
c)   Beta testing
d)   Acceptance testing
e)   Functional testing
f)   Performance testing
g)   Regression testing
h)   Non-functional testing
i)   Monkey testing
j)   Adhoc testing
k)   Exploratory testing
l)   Installation testing
m)   Smoke testing
n)   Volume testing
o)   Stress testing
p)   Load testing
q)   Recovery Testing
r)   Sanity testing
s)   Penetration Testing
t)   Scripts Testing
u)   Loop Testing
v)   Requirements testing
w)   Modules Testing
x)   Destructive testing
y)   Usability testing
z)   Mutation Testing
aa)   Reliability testing
bb)   Graphical User interface testing
cc)   Security testing
dd)   Accessibility testing

ee) Development testing
ff) Big-bang testing
gg) Vulnerable testing
hh) Internationalization and localization testing
ii) Array Testing
jj) Structural testing
kk) Partition testing
ll) Random testing
mm) Data flow testing
nn) Syntax testing
oo) Conformance testing
pp) End to End testing (Work flow testing)
qq) Automation testing
rr) Cosmetic testing

43: What is positive and negative testing?
Answer:
Software testing is a process of Verification and Validation. We need to give some input and check if the resulting output is as per the requirement document. Testing of application is carried out in two ways, Positive testing and Negative testing, which finds out defects in the code.
Positive Testing:
In this testing, the system is validated for valid input data. Which means an input is given to check for a valid set of values which the system should accept as per the expected inputs. The intention of checking this is that the software application should show an error message when it is supposed to and should not show an error message when it's not supposed to. The intention is keeping a positive point of view and only executing positive scenario test cases. This approach of testing is to prove that a given product always meets the requirement specifications.
Negative Testing:
In this testing, test cases are written and tested to ensure that the application can elegantly handle, invalid inputs from the user or unexpected behavior from the user. For example, if a user tries to

type a number in an alphabetic field or text box, the system should display a message to read as "The data type you entered is incorrect. Please only enter alphabets, numeric is not allowed" message. The main purpose of negative testing is to prevent applications from crashing. This type of negative testing helps control users' behavior and shows user friendly quality.

44: What testing types do you carry out for a constrained deadline and why?

Answer:

A planned test strategy may not always work in certain situations. A product needs to be released or should go live for various business factors. There can be demand for end users buying online offers or banking online system or a new product launch or health camps online detail form filling or School Admissions online application form filling for a limited duration or online examination tests with the duration set or online stock market and so on. These deadlines are constrained and requirements may change. The product will be developed first with less time for testing. In such situations, prioritizing testing type is important. Best testing methods should provide with the best results. The aim is to find major possible bugs or defects with a limited time frame. Some 'testing types' that can be followed are:

a) End to End testing can be implemented

b) System testing – selecting major functionality flow for testing

c) Identifying business critical features for testing

d) Reducing focus on component level testing

e) Testing features that are exposed to end users like usability testing

f) Testing features that are developed by a new developer in team

g) Testing those features that are modified or additionally added

h) Testing features that uses new software designing

45: What is boundary value analysis?
Answer:
Boundary value analysis is one of a software testing technique. Test cases are designed to check only the boundary value's ability. The test is to ensure that an error should not occur at the boundaries of a numerical input value. This is because there is a possibility of errors occurring at the extreme ends. Clearly, this testing technique does not concentrate at the centre of the input value.

Consider a text box which requires any numerical input values from 18 to 60. Here, the minimum and the maximum values are tested for errors. The minimum value is 18 and maximum value is 60.

There are three possible ways to test this.
   a) Error should not occur with the input digits itself, 18 and 60.
   b) Errors should not occur for lower values of extreme digits, 18 and 60. Input digits for test case execution will be 17 and 59.
   c) Errors should not occur for greater values of extreme digits, 18 and 60. Input digits for test case execution will be 19 and 61.

Therefore, when an input is entered by the user as, 18, 60, 17, 59, 19 and/or 61; validation message should be thrown to read as 'This is an invalid input data'. Boundary value analysis testing is a part of functionality testing, which falls under black box testing phase. This testing is also known as negative testing and/or stress testing.

46: What is an equivalence class partitioning?
Answer:
Equivalence class partitioning is another software testing technique. This method is used as an effective technique to reduce the number of test cases to a definite class and still covering the maximum requirements. In another sense, test cases are written

into 3 definite categories, where one testable value is picked from each category. When test case is executed for all three categories, one of the output result will be a 'pass' while other two output results will 'fail'. This is called as an equivalence class.
Consider a text box which requires values from 1 to 10 to be accepted. According to this analysis, test cases for all the digits from 1 to 10 as input values need not be written and executed. This test case will have the tester pick a digit between 1 to 10 (including the end digits) and the result should be a 'pass' when the system accepts the value. And another test case is when a user inputs digits outside 1 to 10 as 0, -1,-2 or 11, 12, 13 are said to 'fail' as invalid input data and an appropriate message is thrown. Thus, this kind of testing technique reduces the time taken for executing each and every test case.
Equivalence class partitioning testing is also a part of functional - black box testing phase.

47: What is globalization testing?
Answer:
The market today is competitive; clients from all over the world are spreading globally with technology.
This means an application needs to have global settings like functionality, view ability in cross-browsers, view ability in multiple platforms and readability. By using all possible international inputs, Globalization testing checks for proper functionality of the product with respect to culture or locale settings.
Globalization testing is checking for codes to handle international support without violating functionality in a way not to lose data or display problems. The input should accept all the language texts. The application is first localized & then tested for locale timings and settings, language, content, and interoperability.
Some of the steps to follow for testing are:
  a) Deciding the priority of each module
  b) Selecting a Test platform
  c) Creating the test environment

d) Executing test cases
e) Recognizing the problems and correcting them as required.

The important testing types that are involved are acceptability, compatibility, usability, reliability apart from functionality. These tests, check whether the application is ready for worldwide users. This testing is also known as Internationalization testing.

48: What is alpha and beta stage testing?
Answer:
Alpha and Beta testing stages are an essential mechanism of the overall software testing process to ensure that the software is free of faults and bugs.
Alpha stage testing is the first stage of software testing after the development is done. The term 'Alpha' identifies the stage at which the testing is performed in the testing life cycle and is not yet ready for deployment. The testing is done to perform verification purpose and user acceptance testing. The goal is to check, if the project meets requirement specifications.
It is performed by developers at the development site in a virtual environment. It may sometimes be performed independently by Testers. Alpha stage means, testing performed on application or project within the organization. The real end users are absent in this testing. This is pre deployment phase testing. It is both White box and black box testing categories.
Beta stage testing is done when software passes the Alpha stage testing. Here, a software product is tested rather than the project or application. The term 'Beta' identifies that the product has come to the final deployment stage and is ready to use by the end users.
The testing is performed by end users at their own locations or site by using customer data. The people who are involved in this stage of testing are Test manager/head or Sales Head or Client, End user and/or, Product team. This testing is also the form of Acceptance testing and is always performed outside the organization. The

environment in which the testing is performed is known as real time environment or production environment. Beta testing is open to the market and the public and therefore is also called as field testing. This is only a black box testing category.

49: Is there any difference between retesting and regression?
Answer:

Retesting Testing	Regression Testing
Retesting is done to ensure test cases that produced defects in the last execution are fixed and is passed.	Regression testing is done to ensure when changes like defect fixes, enhancements to the module or application, updating additional features, do not affect the whole application or product. That is the unchanged portion of the application is not affected.
Retesting is carried out when a defect is fixed.	Regression testing is carried out as planned for the specific area or complete testing.
Retesting is done for the test cases which failed earlier in older build.	Regression testing can be done for test cases which passed earlier in older build.
Retesting test cases cannot be prepared before test execution of older fixed defects. Therefore, there is no specific document followed.	Regression test cases are derived from the user manuals, the functional specification documents, defect reports and tutorials in relation to corrected problems.
Retesting has a defect verification process.	Regression testing does not have a defect verification process.

Retesting Testing	Regression Testing
Automation is not possible for the test cases under Retesting, because only fixed defects are tested. Hence automation cannot be considered.	Automation is possible and is the right time for regression testing. Regression testing that is carried out manually, will be expensive with each new release and is time consuming. Hence automation can be opted when the system is considered stable.
Retesting is prioritized over Regression testing, so defects fixed are tested out before regression testing.	Regression testing can be carried out in parallel with Retesting depending upon the availability of the resources.

50: What is a checklist? How is it part of Quality?

Answer:

Every industry employs QA or QC or Quality management as per the industry standards. The checklist is a part of the quality checking process. A checklist in general term means a list of items to check for existence and coverage in a step by step procedure. It contains 'To Do and Not to Do' inspection items to be checked. A Checklist can be called as a tool for measuring quality performance. This kind of a checklist is widely used for many business projects. A Checklist can be created or designed for almost any process, small or big. It ensures there is nothing missing out from the system. This is a necessary portion to ensure a smooth process and quality delivery to the client. In Software testing, checklist can be created at various stages.

    a) **Checking scripts assigned**

        This is always the first step to follow. Scripts are assigned to testers based on the daily workload or based on understanding skills.

b) Checking Test report tool for status of the defect
This is the next important step for the checklist. A Bug report tool is used to keep track of the status of bugs assigned, work in progress and fixed by the developer. The Tester then re-tests and closes the bug to see that the bug is successfully resolved.

c) Checklist is written for executing scripts
Test cases written in a Test template are executed and actual results are entered and then compared and prioritized.

d) Checklist is written for logging defects
Defects are logged with the help of a tool. Developers fix the defects and assigned them to testers for retesting. Resolved defects are closed.

An email is sent to the Team lead with the daily work status report, as per the above checklists for various stages. The report should contain, No. of scripts executed, No. of defects raised, Comments added on defects and queries.

51: Write checklist for script execution.
Answer:
This kind of a checklist is to generally help not lose any process related steps and prevent errors committed by the tester. This is a critical process for a tester. The checklist steps to take care will be:

a) Getting complete details and update the test data document with fields like, Username, test code, functionality.

b) As per the testing standards, using appropriate naming convention to identify a bug.

c) Updating test reporting tool with scripts being executed in the tool.

d) Providing clear test data used by the tester while testing and taking relevant screen shots for any bugs found. Taking Screen shots into a word document is a must, as a proof of finding bugs.

e) Updating bug management tool with status like bug status, severity, time found, date found, name of the tester and so on. This is a part of bug life cycle.

f) Updating the daily or weekly tracking sheets with respect to 'test reporting tool status', 'bug reporting status' and more.

g) Re-checking done to ensure all the scripts are executed properly and test report tool is updated accordingly.

h) The last and final important step for the day is to have a peer review. To ensure a tester does not miss any process during the test case execution stage.

52: Write the checklist for defects logging.

Answer:

Defects logging is the crucial step of a test execution phase. Defects are simultaneously logged while test execution is done, using MS office or a tool as per the organization standards. This is done before submitting defects to the developers. The checklist at this stage helps in the smooth process of logging defects.

a) When a defect is found, checking with the senior or test lead for a valid defect is necessary.

b) Defects are logged in the tool with proper naming convention; this is to ensure that the defect is clearly understood.

c) Attaching appropriate screen prints for the defects with clear descriptions, and additional information given, if needed.

d) Getting reviewed by a senior or team lead for checking details of defect entered in the tool before hitting the submit button.

e) Submitting defects by clicking on send button or submit button.

f) Making note of Defect ID (unique number) and updating the test track sheet/defect track sheet with information.

g) A good backup with all the defect details as above should be maintained.

53: What is blocking and unblocking of scripts? Provide its checklist.
Answer:
A particular test script is said to be blocked in a given scenario, when a potential bug has occurred and due to which further scripts cannot be executed. The further scripts are blocked until the bug is resolved. After the confirmation of the resolved bugs, the blocked script is unblocked. This means the further test scripts can then be executed for testing purpose. The checklists to be followed are:

a) Confirming the bug by reproducing it and then take screen shots of the bug if possible.

b) Confirming with senior or test lead that further scripts are not executable due to the bug.

c) Raising the bug to the developers

d) Updating defect status as: New

e) Once the developers confirm the bug and change the defect status to: assigned, fixed and resolved.

f) Updating the defect in the reporting tool and tracking documents with Defect ID.

g) Retesting for resolved bug if it is working fine.

h) If resolved, continuing further with executing the blocked scripts and thus unblocking it.

54: How is a Test case executed?
Answer:
Test cases are written with a test template. A test template is a format usually in MS Excel sheet. Test modules are developed and test scenarios are identified. Each Test scenario has set of test cases written.

Testers start executing the test cases one by one, and make notes in the sheet with actual results. Relevant screen shots are taken to give a clear understanding of the defect. Steps are also provided to inform developers as to how the test was executed. This method also acts as a proof for testers. Testers can provide with additional information like, input data selection, procedures, and understanding of functionality. This helps developers identify issues easily and fix the defect.

Test reporting tool and bug reporting tool is updated as required. The test tracking sheet is also updated with relevant information by testers. During the above process, checklists are implemented to ensure that all procedures are carried out successfully by the testing team members. This is the process of test case execution.

55: How to perform Exploratory or Adhoc testing?
Answer:
Exploratory testing is a state when there is no proper requirement document. This is an informal testing process which does not have a plan and schedule. Since there is no plan, there are no test cases. Here, testers go by exploring the software to know and understand the nature and purpose of the design. The functionality is also understood. Hence it's name as Exploratory testing. In this process, designing the test cases is simultaneously done by executing them. Test scenarios are created based on the understanding of the software or application. This test challenges the skills and capability of a tester.

After that, start actual testing of application. Other situations where Exploratory testing is carried on is when there is minimum or incomplete requirement specifications; when there is no time or less time to test the application; and when early stage application testing is done.

There are a few things to remember while exploratory testing is to check for limitation of the application; scaling the project and performing exhaustive testing. This testing is also known as Adhoc testing.

56: What is Functional testing and Non-functional testing?
Answer:
The testing that checks for the functioning of the application; when the user performs an action, the application should respond correctly with a reaction. There is functional specification written for the whole application that needs to be covered, this testing is

performed to ensure it validates as per the specification. This is known as Functional testing. Ex: Clicking on 'Home' tab, should take the user to new page with details/purpose of the application (website).

The testing that is not part of functional specifications and concentrates on issues like recovery, reliability, scalability and volumes is known as Non-functional testing. This testing checks for the behavior of the application for a given situation. This testing is said to be successful when the application does not crash, or no loss of data or behaves exactly the same way as suppose to under additional stress or volumes. Ex: Checking of application with workload (data volumes) given more than the defined limit and see if the application is stable. Another instance, check the network speed by using more data in the application and record the response to be the same.

57: What is Performance testing and how is it useful?
Answer:
A Non-functional testing is also known as Performance testing. Under performance testing, it can be done to check various factors like:

a) Comparing two applications to see which one performs better.
b) Measuring which part of the application is performing badly.
c) Measuring how much workload the system can tolerate.
d) Measuring time taken to give the output
e) Checking the speed of the application
f) Checking for loss of data, when the application abruptly loses out power connections.

There are tools used to perform this testing like Load runner, Win runner, Web load, Neoload, Rational performance tester, and so on. Performance testing is very useful to check mobile applications, server response, students taking online exams and so. Other uses related to technical testing are, intention to have a good user experience on web applications and sites, better database configuration, check if a release is ready for production and check if increased revenue generation is possible from websites. This testing can also be called as behavioral testing.

58: What is Monkey testing?
Answer:
It is the user or tester behaving with the intensions of a monkey for testing. It is a unit test and there are no specific tests outlined. In this testing process, the monkey is supposed to produce an input and feed to the system. The resultant output is recorded. Example: Entering random strings (nouns) into text boxes; entering all possible user inputs like 'alphanumeric, special characters or other language characters, junk characters'. Another can be by providing input with rubbish files (Word or Excel) for loading in unrealistic data. This is called as monkey test. There are many monkey testing types, they are, Smart and Dumb Monkeys. Monkey testing is used for automated testing with tools to serve the purpose. Smart monkey testing is used for stress and load testing (data upload and pull). Dumb monkey testing is used to detect for crashes or hangs which is considered as major to fix in an application. While Smart monkey results in a large number of bugs, Dumb monkey results in important but less bugs.

59: Explain Installation testing, Sanity and Smoke testing.
Answer:
Testing the process of installing and uninstalling an application or a software of a system. A test engineer identifies what a customer must do when a software is expired or a new software needs to be added to existing systems. The setup may involve full or partial installations or upgrading software processes. This testing may need configuration management skills. Checking the system with respect to hardware configuration specifications is known as **Installation testing**.
Immediately after a software is built, testers perform smoke testing. As the name suggests, it is to identify any major breaks in

the system soon after the build is ready. A **Smoke testing** is the technique of verifying all the basic mechanisms of a software system are functioning properly. This is also referred to as a quick-dirty testing, to know if major functions of a software piece are working properly. The traditional saying is that the system in this testing technique should not 'catch on fire'.

The Testing team performs **Sanity Testing** to determine if a new software version is ready for a major testing process like automation or load or stress testing. It is one time testing process and test cases are written to check major and critical functionality of the application. It is to check the readiness of the system for further testability.

60: Explain Stress, Volume and Load testing.
Answer:
Stress testing is a testing method, where the system is put under certain conditions that are above its limits. The conditions for checking are met beyond the manual working nature of the system. When the limitation point is reached, the results are examined for further product decision making or enhancements if any. This kind of testing determines the stability of the entire product.

Example: Internal components such as memory, processor utilization, disk space (should not crack unexpectedly), connections and data.

Load Testing, can be called as a division of Stress testing. This stage of testing verifies if a web site can handle a set of parallel users while maintaining suitable response time. That is observing what happens, when multiple users login to a system at the same time or if it can handle the expected amount of load. This is called as **Load testing**.

As the naming suggests, Volume testing refers to testing a system for a certain amount of data and checking its performance. The data is in terms of volumes like a database size or the size of an interface file. Data can also be in an Excel file or MS access and so on.

Example: There is a requirement for the application to interact with an interface file like .dat or .xml, to read/write from or on the file; so a sample file is created with the expected size and testing is done to check the functionality of the application and its performance. This is known as **Volume testing.**
All the above testing types belong to non-functional technique.

61: Explain Usability and Mutation testing.
Answer:
The testing performed, as Usability, is to check if the application interface is user friendly. The aim is to know the usability of the software. The application should be easy to use and understandable. The main aspects to investigate are: efficiency, memorable, error free, learnable and satisfying. The application should be accessible from the layman point of view. User manuals, User Guide, flexible and clean directions to use the web, and clear instructions, are the features of this testing. This is **Usability testing**.
The method of testing, which involves modifying program's byte code or source code in minute ways is known as **Mutation testing**. The mutated code which is not identified and discarded by the test suite; such a test suite is considered defective. Therefore, a good test suit should identify the mutated (false) code and is said to be successful. The process of inserting faulty codes into programs in order to determine whether the test suit picks these faults is known as Mutation Testing. Once the mutation is found or caught by the tests, it is killed. This method facilitates the tester develop effective tests or locate weaknesses in the test data. This also helps identify data that are never used in test execution. Mutation testing is the form of Structural testing.

62: Explain Array testing and API testing.
Answer:
Array testing is also known as Orthogonal Array testing. It is a black box testing technique that is a carried out methodically and the statistical way of software testing. The number of inputs used

in the system is comparatively low. It is mostly useful in finding errors connected with logical faults within software systems. And every probable input cannot be used in the systems for exhaustive testing. Since this is a statistical way of testing, the permutation or combination of issue levels containing a single treatment is carefully chosen such that, the responses are not coincidental. In this situation each treatment provides a distinctive bit of info. The experiments are conducted in a minimum number with the same piece of data being gathered. Array testing can be tried for regression testing, configuration testing, system testing, performance testing, and user interface testing.

API is the acronym for Application Programming Interface. It is a collection of program subroutines and procedures called as API calls. This can be executed by other software applications. Other application's code uses these APIs for their functionality. Therefore, API acts as a link and is known as a web service provider. This link is flawless. The testers test this framework with a test harness application that links with the API. This application systematically practices its functionality by constructing a copy in a way that end users might use the application. This process is known as **API testing**.

63: Explain Cosmetic and Syntax testing.
Answer:
Cosmetic testing involves checking for errors caught by eyes usually on a web page. When a user is looking into a web, consistency in the Font colours, Font sizes, Background colour, line breaks, text alignments and spelling errors or grammar mistakes; Table colours and alignment; Tab or Button colours, should all meet the requirement throughout the application. Any inconsistency or deviation from the expected requirement constitutes for fixing by the developers. These conditions usually arise when there is an enhancement with respect to GUI design in the application. Therefore testing is concentrated only around the changes or enhancement requirements. The finding of differences mentioned above is known as **Cosmetic testing**.

Syntax Testing is performed in a White Box Testing technique. This testing may use some tools or may be manually performed, depending on the nature of the task. In most cases, developers prefer automation for this type of testing. In this process, the developers run a syntax check before releasing their program code to the software testing team. Criteria for testing may vary from one organization to the other and the general steps are: Identifying target language (like C++, Java, .Net, C Sharp), defining the syntax, and validating and debugging the syntax. This test can also be done by white box testers depending on the arrangement. A test case design technique that involves testing a component or system input is known as **Syntax testing**.

64: What are Localization testing and Isolation testing?
Answer:
Localization means transforming the product's user interface and making changes with some settings to suit local language or region. Localization testing means checking the quality of a product's localization aspects like culture or local. This testing can be executed only on the localized environment. The main features that come under testing are User Interface, and content such as Currency, Tax, Region and Language. Note that, sometimes the design may change with functional features to adjust the application as per the respective country. Other tests that should be performed as part of the localization is, Functionality testing, Configuration/Installation testing based on that region language support, and Compatibility testing. Based on the above and globalization, testing that verifies the functionalities for that particular culture is called as **Localization testing**.
Isolation testing is kind of similar to performance testing. The process of repeating a test execution to prove the existence of a defect in a system by isolating is known as **Isolation testing**.
In other words, modules are broken down to sub modules that are isolated, so that flaws can be seen easily. This testing is utilized when a bug or defect is difficult to locate and resolve. Since it is time consuming, stubs or drivers are used to test each module

separately.

65: What is Soak testing and Fuzz testing?
Answer:
Soak testing means checking the performance of a system in depth for a long period to examine any potential discrepancy. The system is run under high loads for 12 or 24 hrs continuously during a heavy traffic. Here load refers to time. There may be performance issues after extending long period communication with the system. Some STLC process may also use soak testing for months with high temperatures or external stresses.
Example: A system behaves normally when tested for a couple of hours. But, when it is tested beyond two hours, problems like 'memory leakage' may arise and the system will fail or act unexpectedly.
Fuzz testing is also a Black box testing technique. Using bad data randomly to attack a code and observing breaks in the system is known as Fuzz testing. Automation is done for effective results of Fuzz testing of large applications. This kind of testing ensures the best practice for the application, is well protected.

66: What is End to End testing and Compatibility testing?
Answer:
Every application has a beginning and end towards a completed product. This testing involves testing carried from first to last with major functionality being covered. The method of testing the flow of an application to perform as designed from first to last is known as **End to End testing.**
The need for testing is to check system dependencies and if there is a correct communication passed between components and systems. The communicating components are database, networking, hardware and other applications. This testing is similar to system testing where a complete coverage leads to end to end checking. It is important to perform this testing in a production environment or parallel live environment.
The application or a software is tested on different interfaces like

browsers, peripherals, hardware platforms, Operating systems, Database and more. This testing is also a part of behavioral testing and is used to check the stability of the application with external factors other than the application itself. Below are the detailed components considered for testing.

a) Web based applications are tested on browsers and the elements included are Netscape, Google Chrome; Internet explorer and its versions; Firefox and its versions, Opera, and Safari.

b) Peripherals interface testing includes, DVD drive, Printers, Scanners and more. Database included are SQL server, Oracle, Sybase and more.

c) Operating systems interface are: Windows, Unix, Linux, etc.

d) The other software application interface is: Web server, Messaging tool, and more.

This software external factor testing is known as **Compatibility testing.**

67: Explain Reliability, Recovery and Security testing.
Answer:
Reliability Testing: The application is tested to see if it is reliable. This is a performance based testing. The testing is done at the early stage to detect if there are any problems with the design and is trustable.
Recovery Testing: This testing is also a performance based testing. It is used to verify a software application restarts after a failure has occurred and that data is not lost. The crashes of an application or a software occurs due to hardware failures or major network disconnection or router issues. The application must be stable enough to cope up with such crashes and this is known as Recovery testing.
Security testing: This testing is a part of performance testing. Security testing can be for any or all of the following needs:

a) Testing done to determine User information confidentiality like 'User input name, password, and

Email ID'.

b) Testing carried to determine that an information system protects user data and maintains functionality as intended. Ex: An application which has user bank details with respect to personal accounts, salary, transaction details, and more.

c) Testing carried to check, that a system is protected against unauthorized internal and external access. Ex: Malicious software introduced, hacking a system by introducing a piece of code and Virus attacks through networks.

Thus, Security testing is the process to determine Authenticity, Security, Encryptions, and Authorization in a software application.

68: What are Gorilla testing and Scalability testing?
Answer:

Gorilla Testing: Gorilla Testing involves testing a particular module with all aspects by testers or developers. Only one module functionality is considered for testing it heavily. These test cases are executed extensively as part of manual testing process for several times to check robustness of the application. Therefore, it is a monotonous (heavy) testing type and poses a challenge to a tester. A tester must avoid this boredom to ensure he does not miss out on a possible error. Basically, this testing is different from Monkey Testing and Random Testing.

Scalability Testing is to test if the non-functioning of a system are capable of meeting the volume and size changes as per the requirements. In this testing, environment settings are kept constant and load testing is done with various software and hardware configurations which are updated for each test execution. Ex: Tools are used in order to test parallel connections, user loads, many internet service's throughputs and other transactions.

69: What are GUI testing and Spike testing?
Answer:
A GUI testing is performed to assure the user perspective of an application or a software. A user must feel right about the looks and accessibility (as in a web browser). The user must get clarity to use the application and should hook to the application. It concentrates on keyboard and mouse events such as scroll bars, navigations like 'back' or 'home page' button, Menu bars, tool bars, dialogs, message box, Text fields, list box, validation box, buttons, pictures, pictures and more. GUI means Graphical user Interface and Graphics represent images, pictures, icons and attractive features on a web page. Testing conducted to ensure the functionality with respect to the above elements is known as **GUI testing**.

Testing conducted to observe the behavior of the system by a sudden increase in the number of users or increasing the load by a very large amount. The goal is to determine if the system fails or handles the remarkable changes in load. Spike testing should ensure that the system functions appropriately after resuming back from a spike activity. This is known as **Spike testing**. Spike testing is a form of load testing, but spike checks for sudden activities and responses.

70: Give examples for load and spike testing.
Answer:
Load testing examples can be as follows:
  a) A large number of files are downloaded from the internet
  b) A printer is assigned a series of tasks in a queue
  c) Heavy amounts of email traffic are loaded in the server
  d) Multiple server applications are simultaneously run on a server
Spike testing examples can be as follows:
  a) When a fire alarm testing is done in a corporate building, all the employees are evacuated. They resume back to work after the testing is completed. They all log in around the same time and the servers undergo sudden loads.

b) During power cut problems if there is no backup power system, all employees face sudden shutdown of the computers and servers. Once the power is back, all employees log in at the same and the server is sluggish due to heavy loads in a less period of time.

c) A new system or a fresh version of a product is released to production and users simultaneously access the product with a short period of time

d) When an internet service or other system breakout happens, all users lose access to their system. Once the breakout has been set, users log into the system at the same time.

71: What is Encryption, Authentication and Authorization in testing?
Answer:
Security testing ensures for Authentication, Authorization and Encryption.

a) **Encryption**: Encryption is the conversion of data like, credit card statements, phone number, society security number, date of birth, address, and more. This sensitive information is converted into an undetectable code called as cipher text that will not be understood by unauthorized people. In this way, private and useful data of a person are secured on the web. This can again be converted back to its original data through another process called as Decryption. This is a major security check in the STLC world as more and more people are becoming internet savvy as efficient and effective substitutes of managing daily chores. Information can be private and needs to be protected from theft, thus Encryption acts as police on the internet.

b) **Authentication**: Authentication is the process of creating logins for a person, a device, a process, a system, an object, or a component for identification. The individuality of a person is based on a username and password or an ID

(Identity) number and so on. This piece of information (username, password, email ID, Security number, etc.) is used for confirmation of the basic identity being claimed. This whole process is known as Authentication.

c) **Authorization**: Authorization is followed by Authentication process. It is a process of granting permission to use a system or application or a component by using the username and password or ID. It is the accessing rights given to an individual, a process, an object, or a device, over restricted resources for a given period of time.

72: How is Benchmark testing done?

Answer:

A benchmark is the pace of running a number of standard tests of computer programs or other operations, in order to analyze the performance. Benchmark testing is the process of load testing under which a component or a whole system (end to enare tested to conclude the performance features of the application. The tests are duplicated and the measurements of performance captured, vary a little every time. This allows changes updated particularly in the application to determine if there is a performance improvement. Benchmark testing can also merge with aspects of security testing.

Benchmark testing can be explained with an example of installing firewalls. Firewall testing requires system loads or user loads pooled with implementing security violation criteria's, simultaneously executed against the component to evaluate its benchmark performance.

There are two types of benchmark testing objectives; to examine the system and measure how a change can affect its performance descriptions; to try and adjust the system and reach a service level agreement or requirement. In this case a series of benchmark tests are carried along with iterative cycles of performance modification.

73: Give examples of stress testing.
Answer:

    a) A web server or web site is stressed using bots, scripts, and various service tools and performance is observed under peak loads.

    b) A computer system with adequate memory is run with numerous applications simultaneously without difficulty. By introducing a hacker or virus, the system might crash and close. Therefore, stress testing is done to ensure a security criteria are met.

    c) Pushing identified transactions to greater levels and checking for breakup in transactions or in systems is another example.

    d) A few selected transactions are highly stressed with fewer loads on the database.

    e) A case with Internet Explorer to check its ability to handle crashes, while many users or one user opens many IE browser instances of a website. Trying to lock one instance should still allow other instances to work normally.

    f) Large amount of data is input (uploaded) to the software or application through excel or database to test the speed (time taken to treat a particular functionality or command by the user) and observe for any bugs or for hanging up.

74: Explain the state of UAT testing.
Answer:

UAT means User acceptance Testing. This stage of testing is the last stage in the STLC process. It is carried out from the user perspective and is done just before the final release. The people involved here are a couple of key stakeholders like Tester or Sales head or Project Manager or the client or customer. This testing is done to ensure the product or software is ready to be delivered to the client or deployed to the production and that all the potential defects are resolved. Some of the checkpoints of testing UAT as per the standards of Microsoft are,

    a) System Menu should have Exit or Close options in the

form of buttons
b) Labelling (naming) must not overlap
c) All controls must be aligned properly
d) Every label name should begin with an uppercase alphabet
e) All commands must be clearly visible with very relevant names.
f) Compulsory use of OK and Cancel option buttons
g) The appropriate message box should be in place

These are very important check points in GUI testing. The above rules are part of User Interface testing.

75: Define the term 'Vulnerability' and its use in testing.
Answer:
Vulnerability is related to the security in the computer world. The term vulnerability is the weakness of the system that allows an attacker to reduce its information or data assertion. There are three elements of checking Vulnerability.
a) A system's flaw
b) An attacker's potential to take advantage of the flaw
c) An attacker's admission to the flaw

To create a vulnerable system, an attacker uses at least one appropriate tool or skill that can connect to a system's weakness. Vulnerability is the attacking surface and the attackers may use any of the following ways to attack.
a) An attacker can execute commands as another user.
b) An attacker can collect information
c) An attacker may deny service
d) An attacker behaves as another unit

When a system vulnerability is completely attacked with one or more known occasion of working is considered as an exploit. The time from when the security crack was manifested into deployed software, to when access was removed and a security fix was available or the attacker was disabled; is known as the period of vulnerability.

76: Explain Testing Limitations.
Answer:
Software testing also has limitations. Based on this limitation, certain realistic expectations are set. The following are some limitations:

a) Testing is a process to rectify errors and is not permanent resolution. Testing can never declare the absence of defects, while it can only find defects.

b) Exhaustive testing is almost impossible.

c) It cannot give any idea about the uncovered defects. Hence, testing cannot promise that the software or application is error free.

d) Sometimes there is compromising with respect to budget and thorough testing.

e) Testing cannot help decide the release of a product or deploy. The decision is based on the business requirement of the client and either the deadline is extended or minor (low priority) defects are pushed to the next release.

f) Testing does not find root causes of defects.

g) Under some circumstances, testing may be incorrect due to ambiguous requirements.

h) Testing can only discover that functionality is not proper under specific conditions.

i) In most cases, testing runs out of time upon completion of test case execution.

77: Explain Test Monitoring.
Answer:
A test monitoring is management task that is related to checking the status regularly with various activities of a test project. The actual results are compared and the results are generated which was planned. Some of the test monitoring purposes during the project is as follows:

a) The project team has to be supplied with clear test results.

b) The test manager and testing team are given feedback on the progress of the testing work, in turn providing opportunities to improve the project and testing.
c) The project team has to collect data useful in calculating test efforts for the future.
d) Determine whether the testing is completed by measuring the status from test entry criteria with that of exit criteria like, coverage of tests and testing items.

In small projects, the test leader or a dedicated member gathers test monitoring information manually by using MS documents and simple databases. But, in large projects or long term testing efforts use automated tools for monitoring information like consistency and efficiency of data collection. Another way of keeping records is by using the IEEE-829 test log template. These are the ways of tracking, testing progress information.

78: Give an example of Integration Testing.
Answer:
Integration testing uses database interactions, external system like a mail server, network, and files to read or write Input and output data. Other examples are:

a) Integration testing on a staging environment, for the CRM (Customer relationship management) to communicate with a printer.
b) Verifying the whole data flow of receiving an order, creating an invoice, saving it to the DB and mailing it to the client. This is known as an End-To-End integration test.
c) Testing a keyboard of a computer when it is combined with the mouse of a computer. To see the coordination of the two devices working together is known as Integration testing.
d) When two individual applications are combined to perform as a whole task, then Integration testing is done to check its complete workflow.

e) When an individual application uses web service application (like flight travel information) to provide end data information to users, then the integration testing is done to ensure smooth communication and data transfer between them.

Thus the pre-requisite of Integration testing is to ensure that unit testing is done for each component.

79: What are Component testing and Configuration testing?
Answer:

Component Testing: A component testing is sometimes also called as unit testing. But this testing involves a higher level of unit testing and is closer to integration testing. This testing considers a whole application instead of a specific module. This testing is performed by developers or testers.

a) It is also a type of program or code (module) testing.

b) Based on the SDLC model chosen, component testing sometimes is done in remote from the rest of the system. In the absence of a software, Stubs and Drivers are chosen as the replacement and simulation are done as an interface between the software modules.

For instance, if there are dependent modules and only one module is developed while other two are not developed; Stub and Driver are used as replacement for another two undeveloped module and tested.

Configuration Testing: Configuration testing technique is carried out to check the hardware and software connections with respect to check their effective communication. Whenever a hardware is added or removed or modified with resources such as disk drives, CPU, and memory, testing is executed to determine the best configuration of the application. This testing is part of performance process and is tested by engineers. This technique is effective when a software is required for different types of users.

80: Give an example of real case testing scenario for Work flow testing.

Answer:

Consider two web based applications, Advertising and Publisher products. They are two individual products with interrelated work flow.

Work Flow Testing: Consider an individual Advertising application. This is an agent that places advertisements of its clients on the publisher's site with their placement criteria. Testing can be performed from the beginning to the end with the work flow related functionality check.

   a) Login to the server with user logins 'Username and Password'
   b) Select the client and sub product.
   c) Check the major modules like 'creating a campaign -> sending an invoice for billing -> inserting the creative -> checking the advertisement on the browser with the URL generated -> sending a mail to the client with the link attached -> perform trafficking to host the link on the server, -> and check for Reports once the advertisement goes live for knowing placement criteria like 'impressions, clicks and click through rates'.
   d) Log out of the application successfully.

The functionality in the above steps should not break and any bugs found relating to these stages are sent for fixing. This ensures the execution of work flow testing.

81: Give a real case testing scenario for Functional testing.

Answer:

Consider two web based applications, advertising agent product. This product hosts advertisement on publisher sites. The process involved are 'selecting a client, selecting sub product, creating a campaign with advertisement placement criteria settings, uploading creative, inserting into campaign, Rotate the campaign and Reports'. Functional testing considers the following,

Functional testing: The above application can have many

modules executed as per the test scripts and one of the small 'login and logout' scenarios can be as follows,

a) Login with a Tester user name and password -> check the page logs in successfully and shows 'Home' page with a list box as 'Client' and names under the list to select. Also the page should show 'Products' labelled dropdown box (is inactive until client name is selected). Also a small top right corner should show the tester/user logged name with label as 'User name' and a 'Logout' button.

b) Select the client name and check for 'Product' dropdown box, should show all the products relevant to that client.

c) Next select the product and find the new page should load to show - > main menu tabs as 'Campaign | Creative | Traffics | Rotation | Reporting' and the 'Logout' button should still be available.

d) Lick on Logout button and check for successful logout page being load with a message to show as 'The user has successfully logged out'.

82: What is a Cookie and why is it used?
Answer:

A Cookie is a small piece of information stored in the text file by the web server. This data usually contains user data that is personalized like Name or email ID. Later, this data is used by browsers (web pages or sites) for communication purposes between web pages or browsers. Essentially, cookies store the user's identity and track the user navigations throughout the browser pages. The communication between a browser and a server is done through the help of cookies, which later is used to capture the users' interest and activities on a particular website. This is used for tracking business performance at the customer's site. Technically, when a user visits the website or web page, a small code from the HTML page is written on a text file of the user's machine and this is called as a cookie.

There are two kinds of cookies in nature:

a) Persistent cookies: Permanently written cookies on a user machine that last for months or years is known as Persistent cookies.

b) Session cookies: Session means some period of time, some time limit, say 30 minutes is set to expire (kill / remove) the cookie. A cookie is active until the browser is open. When the browser is closed, the session cookie is removed.

Cookies are stored in different paths depending on the browser type. Meaning, different browsers have different cookie storage paths. An IE stores cookies on C:\Documents. Cookies are used for various tracking purposes like: Shopping cart, marketing sites, displaying commercial advertisements, personalized web pages, and user tracking session. A user on his system or computer can enable or disable cookie settings, depending on either he wants the data to be stored/tracked or not.

83: How is a Cookie setting carried out?
Answer:
The pre-requisite to check for writing a test case is to ascertain if the cookies are properly written by the application on the computer storage disk. Below are the steps to follow:

a) For some cookie privacy policies, a tester needs to ensure that a user's personal and sensitive data is not stored in the cookie.

b) If sensitive data needs to be stored in cookies, then ensure data stored is in encrypted format.

c) While testing, there should be no excess use of cookies. When a browser often pops up for cookie allowance permission, this will annoy the user from his activity. Therefore, it results in loss of site traffic and ultimately loses business.

d) Some browsers display useful information when cookies are enabled. Therefore, disabling a cookie, might not allow some major site functionalities.

e) Disable a cookie to test the smooth functioning of the page, and no crash of any page should occur due to the act of disabling the cookies.

84: What test cases are written for a Cookie setting?
Answer:
There are many test cases to check cookie functionality and they
are:

a) **Accepting and Rejecting cookies to control the smooth
functionality of a web application:** To test for a good
functionality of a website, all cookies must not be
accepted. The testing should be done by setting browser
options, to prompt when an HTML code wants to write a
cookie to the disk. Divide the cookie acceptance into half
of the size, say 5 accepted randomly and 5 rejected. Then
the window prompts for each cookie to be accepted or
rejected and can be managed accordingly. Now check the
website major functionality to see if data is getting infected
or pages are crumbling.

b) **A Test to check the deletion of cookies from self web
application page:** Testing an action tracking on a web
portal. A pixel is placed on the web page for tracking any
action made by the user or business purchase done; the
cookie tracks the action and/or purchase. While other
testing is being done, to avoid multiple tracking of the
actions logged from the same cookie, the cookie written to
disk is deleted. Therefore, the cookie must be successfully
deleted for our tests.

c) **Test to delete a cookie:** Check by allowing a website to
insert cookies on browsers and then close it. Next, delete
all cookies manually for a website under trial. Now,
reopen the browsers of the web pages and check the
behavior of the pages. In this case, cookies must be
disabled and tracking of data should not happen.

d) **Testing for Cookie on Multiple browsers:** An important
test is to check if one web application page writes the
cookies properly on all or different browsers as planned.
The site should work properly by using these cookies.

Testing is done on major browsers like Internet explorer, Opera, Chrome, Mozilla Firefox, Netscape and more.

e) **Test for corrupt data in the cookie content**: Cookies can be easily corrupted. A cookie is manually edited in a notepad and parameter is changed with some corrupt values for the content or the Name or expiry date. Check the site functionality. Our cookies should not allow reading data of another domain in spite of corrupted cookie.

85: When is a Parallel live testing stage used?
Answer:
A Parallel testing is carried on with the same input data being run on two versions of the same application. When a new version of the system is developed with new features or software as part of new requirements (version); testing the data (old or changed) through the old version application and the new version is known as Parallel testing. Here the old version is live environment setup and hence testing done is on parallel live testing. The other system is used for comparison while old and new versions of the applications are same. Parallel testing is used when there is ambiguity regarding the accuracy of functionality of the new application. It is a method of transferring data to and fro of a previous system to a target system in an IT organization. In order to reduce risk, the new and old systems run simultaneously for some period of time. Once the criteria for the new system are met, the old system will be disabled. There is a good amount of time required for this process with a well laid plan.

86: Elaborate on Game testing and its importance
Answer:
Game testing is simply testing of games online or a dedicated server.

Online games should be tested before they are released to the public, and this testing is a field that requires specific computing and challenging skills. Having a passion to play will be added advantage for testing. There are many types of online games with varied designs. The game application designing is essential and may be tough and hence will be testing.

Computers are becoming powerful and video games gave rise to online games and are also on mobiles. These games are complex in program while making it exciting to play. Games are enjoyed by any age group because of the fact that it is capturing in its looks and design factors like music, colours, and innovativeness in the computer industry. Games are sold in CD format or available online or installed on a computer as a software. There are wide varieties of games available in the market. Games are available with a trial version to decide which game to buy. These games are tested before they are formally released in the market.

As a tester, technical skills may not be required, but surely a flair for catching software bugs in games is needed. Most gaming companies have their own quality assurance department with numerous testers to examine various aspects of each game. Testers need to work closely with gaming programmers to clearly understand the concept of gaming. They also exchange ideas with developers for each trial.

Defects or bugs in a game can cost severe losses to the company in terms of reputation and investment and hence game testing is very important. When a game is going to be launched into the market, resolving last minute bugs also hit on investment and delay in launch, therefore, the proper test plan is necessary.

It is a critical computer industry with games and testing is very challenging and defects or bugs in this case need to be fixed before release.

87: What is Cloud testing?
Answer:

One of the recent kind of testing is Cloud testing based on latest computing technology. This new technology gives access to resources like, Processors, RAM, and files hosted on the web. Cloud Testing means running your tests on a dispersed environment. This environment includes data centre, the cloud

(Amazon EC2), and links that simulate thousands of user levels. Testing is carried on the application across multiple locations. Cloud testing has a high level with three logical models of generating test traffic and they are: outbound testing from outside of the cloud; into the cloud; and from outside the cloud into the cloud. These factors depend on where the target system is hosted and where test traffic begins.

These models have certainly risen above, the role of testing instruments and services. Therefore, one needs to use a mix of tools during this test. The tools available are 'Grinder, and JMeter'. If it is a simple web application, then even 'Apache AB' will work fine. Some business related Clouds are SOASTA, Google Application Engine, Windows Azure, Amazon Web Services, and Force.com.

88: What are examples of security testing?
Answer:
A few examples of security testing to ensure are:
   a)   An ERP (enterprise resource planning) system needs to be secure so that a data entry operator cannot access 'Reports' section.
   b)   Customers purchasing or shopping online must have security for credit card details or savings card details by performing encryption.
   c)   An SQL query does not retrieve actual passwords of its users for custom made software.
   d)   Checking a bank account status online should have security to ensure login details are not misused by some other user.
   e)   A campaign manager of an advertising agent application should only have access to campaigns and not for creative and reports sections.
   f)   The web service application should ensure successful money transfer without loss of money while online transactions for flight bookings or any other services.
   g)   Restriction is provided to users with authorization to only

view a particular feature in an application like Report manager can simply login to view report section, whereas an Admin login can view all features like Reports, Campaigns, Creative and Billing and trafficking.

h) Security access can be provided even within a particular feature say, accessing reports. Authorization for users is given with respect to Writing, Updating (make changes and save) and Reading.

89: What are Binary testing and Branch testing?
Answer:

Binary Portability Testing: The testing technique that tests for portability of an executable application across different system platforms and environments is known as Binary Portability testing. This technique is usually conformed to an ABI (Application Binary Interface) requirement. Testers perform this type of testing. An ABI is a system interface with compiled programs and is used for various hardware architectures. The Binary Portability testing is conducted on different types of software platforms: Mac OS, Windows(x86, X86-64), Linux, Solaris, Java, and Android.

Branch Testing: It is a testing technique for testing by the developer at least once on all branches in the program source code. This ensures that all accessible code is executed and tracked. Every branch is regarded as true or false and is covered for all possible conclusions. This assists in validating the application for all the branches in the code such that even a single branch does not contribute to irregular behavior.

90: What are Breadth testing and Code driven testing?
Answer:

Breadth Testing: This testing technique is performed by testers. Breadth testing considers a test scenario that completely authenticates the functionality of a product, but does not test characteristics in detail. Breadth testing is also a form of integration testing.

In first breadth testing, all the components may be partially developed at the same level of mastery. A combination of the both breadth and depth testing approach can be applied.

These components are first tested in breadth manner, and later all these components would be delivered with consecutive modifications. This will be close to a complete functionality of the product. Hence, depth testing of a component must be performed along with breadth testing.

Code driven Testing: Testing frameworks that permits the execution of unit tests to examine whether different sections of the code are behaving as expected under different circumstances. This testing procedure is known as Code driven testing and is performed by the developers.

The Code driven testing is also known as test driven testing. The single test is first executed, which is enough for a code to fail. Later, a complete test suite, or subsets of tests are executed to increase speed of testing and make certain that the new test fails. The code is restructured to run the new trials. Finally, all tests are executed again. If tests fail, the code is modified, and if pass, the initial steps are repeated for next development entry.

91: What is Benchmark testing?

Answer:

Benchmark testing is a division of the software development life cycle. It is a team coordination process that involves application or software developers, application designers and database administrators. This testing is performed to check present performance and improve the application as required. It requires of writing efficient application code as possible. An additional increase in performance might be realized by modifying the database and adjusting database configuration management parameters. Even application parameters can be corrected to better meet demands (requirements) of the application.

There are two ways of benchmark tests run to identify specific information:

    a)   An application benchmark, tests the same input capacity under faster production conditions.

b) A transactions/second benchmark, determines how many input data can be given to the database manager for a certain limited environmental setup condition.

There is benchmarking done, which involves understanding the database manager, responding under altering conditions. Thereby, test Scenarios are created for real world scenarios such as,

a) The new release or version of the product,
b) Usability and performance,
c) Deadlock handling,
d) Characteristics of transaction rate when more users are being added
e) Loading data with different methods

The key for modifying benchmark configuration parameters are based upon these above factors. This requires running database (SQL or Oracle) repeatedly from the application with different parameters until the application runs efficiently.

92: Explain Cross browser testing and how is it different from compatibility testing.

Answer:

There is a wide range of web browsers available and end users are trying these that best suits them. Thus, it is crucial to test applications on web browsers. Client components like AJAX requests, JavaScript, Applets, Flex, Flash, etc., are used in applications and they behave differently from one browser to another. There is a different browser behavior based on the user instrument received from client browser to how requests are processed on server side. This testing is necessary to ensure web application works fine across multiple browsers and checks for compatibility. The study made and observed for both the server and client side behaviors of the application, and accessed using different web browsers is known as Cross Browser Testing. Cross browser testing is a subset of compatibility testing that assures a web application behaves correctly in several different browsers or browser versions. While this technique concentrates specifically on browsers, Compatibility testing checks for browser and other system applications for any discrepancies. Browser testing considers some of the validations,

a) HTML, XHTML and/or CSS validations
b) JQuery and Ajax functionality
c) Font colour and size validations
d) Page validation for JavaScript actions as enable and/or disable
e) Checking for image alignment
f) Checking for Header and footer sections
g) Page layout is checked in different resolutions (pixels in width and height of the screen)
h) Check for Content alignments like Centre or LHS (left hand side) or RHS (right hand side) alignments
i) Page styles and Date formats validations
j) Check for special characters encoded with HTML character
k) Validation for page zoom in and zoom out functionality

For cross browser testing, repeat these tests on: Different browsers (and latest versions) like Internet explorer, Firefox, Netscape, Google Chrome, Safari and Opera.

93: Explain the meaning of Simulation and its relation with computer testing.
Answer:
Simulation means the replica of something from the real world. In this test, a model is developed first. This model inhabits the key features or behaviors of the physical system or process. The model presents the system and the simulation over time represents the operation of the system. Today, simulation is used in various real life contexts. Simulation is used in, technology for optimized performance, testing, safety engineering, video games, human

systems, education, training and so on. The Computer is the basic means of a model and to study any field of simulation. The study to see how the model system works via computer is the process of simulation. Calculations are made about the behavior of the system by changing variables in the process.

Again under computers, simulation is used in various operations. In testing, a large set of scenarios; both new and old data are copied for better KPI (Key Performance Indicator) analysis. This can give an idea as to how the altering variables impact the business. Executing test scripts or simulations provide feedback on the performance without impacting the original applications. These results are generated in the form of a report. Based on this report and KPI analysis, further business decisions are made.

94: Describe Pilot testing.
Answer:
Pilot Testing: This testing involves group of users' hands on developed product to check for basic functionality, features and look and feel feedback of the product is revealed. This is helpful before the product is completely deployed. It is also to get accustomed to the product with the contents. This nature of testing is controlled with a short period of time and the extent of testing depends on the size and reach of the task. Larger projects have a carefully planned testing, that can have stages of pilot testing implemented to suit their demands. The beginning point is before the actual pilot testing is performed and is carried out by key developers for technical aspects. The other stage is actual pilot testing, once the pre pilot stage is done. There are some factors considered during pilot operation,

a) The roll out plan to prepare systems for pilot testing and for deploying the server is executed.
b) Installation documentation is managed.
c) Set up communication modes for efficient handling of corrections if any.
d) Pilot performance evaluation with information and feedback and implement as required.

This is likewise known as Beta stage testing.

95: Describe Penetration testing.

Answer:

Penetration Testing: Penetration testing is testing how well the system is protected against unauthorized internal or external access, or stubborn damage. This case of testing usually requires sophisticated testing techniques.

A penetration test is a method of assessing the security of a computer network or system by reproducing an attack by a malevolent user, known as a cracker (not a hacker). The process requires a dynamic analysis of the system for any possible vulnerability that may result from

  a) Inadequate or improper system configuration,
  b) Known and/or unknown hardware or software flaws,
  c) Operational weaknesses in process,
  d) Technical surveillance countermeasures.

This analysis is considered from the point of an attacker, and may actively engage misuse of security vulnerabilities. The owner will be presented with the system along with an evaluation of whatever security issues are found. The evaluation is based on the impact caused and a proposal given for technical solution or improvement. The intention of a penetration test is to determine the possibility of an attack if disclosed and the amount of business impact if an exploit is successful. The tasks involved are,

  a) Until the security vendor provide the appropriate solution, known / unknown vulnerabilities fight against the threat
  b) Business Risks: Personal information modification, price-list modification, Everyday threat analysis, unauthorized funds transfer, unauthorized logins, breach of customer trust and more.
  c) Technical vulnerabilities: Web application risks, SQL injection, URL manipulation, Cross site scripting, password in memory, session hijacking (cookies should be

in encrypted format and not be stored in browser), back end authentication, web server configuration, credential management, buffer overflow, and more.

96: Describe Documentation testing, Ramp testing and Scripted testing.
Answer:

The nature of testing to check for documents in the form of guides to help users (User guide) understand the application is known as **Documentation testing**. The documentation can be the form of 'requirement specifications' before developing a software for the end client. It can be used for Installation purposes as Installation guide. These are usually kept in a simple form, clear and complete ways.

Increasing an input signal constantly until the system crashes is known as **Ramp testing**. It is conducted by the performance engineer or the testing team. This method helps study the ability of the system capacity when it has a gradual increase in workload. This is also a part of Load testing.

Test cases that need to be developed before test execution and producing some responses as the results are expected to be shown and is known as scripted testing. These test cases are designed by someone experienced and performed by a tester.

97: What are Comparison testing and Pair testing?
Answer:

Comparison testing and Pair testing are two different scenarios of testing and are effective.

As the word comparison, **comparison testing** means comparing one system / software with another superior or a challenging system. Testing is basically concentrated of software comparison with respect to the performance of the software. For instance, testing is done to compare a PDF file converter which is a 'Desktop Based Application' with that of another tough software convertor competitor. The aspects of comparison will be, checking of the speed of conversion of PDF file to word, checking for speed of word converted to PDF file format and Converted file quality maintained.

Pair Testing: In an SDLC, the technique that allows two users to use the same computer, keyboard or system to work together and perform testing of the application is known as Pair testing. In this method, one tester executes the test cases and another tester review's and analyzes the testing. This can be an effective method as the thought process of both the testers help towards good test results. The test execution can be exchanged turn by turn while exchanging ideas and comments and the goal to achieve is the same. These tests can be executed between a Tester and a Developer, or a Business Analyst.

98: Explain Passive testing and Data driven testing.
Answer:
Passive Testing: This testing technique involved in monitoring the results of a working system without introducing any special test data is known as Passive testing. This testing process is performed by the testing team. It consists of following a script in order to get information about the software. All the question and answers are put down for the test. If a single mechanism rupture, the plan will become outdated instantly. These scripted tests are dealt in mass testing, with laid out procedures on how and what to handle. It costs less by testing in this manner, since testers do not need to appoint their brains, and they don't need to think. They just need to read and follow up. It is like shutting down the human brain, and just banging the keys.

Data driven testing: It is the testing done in software, using conditions inserted in a table directly as testing inputs and outputs are verifiable. It also checks for the process not being hard coded with regard to test control and environment settings. The inputs provided by the tester are in a row in the table. The expected outputs also occur in the same row as inserted. The table contains values which match up to equivalence partition or boundary value input sections. These tests can also contain positive and negative tests, which verify if the input data holds true lying inside or outside the boundaries. This way, you can test how the application handles various inputs without having a lot of similar tests which waste time testing manually by checking each field in a database. The data fields are data pools, ADO objects, CSV (comma separated value) files, ODBC sources, DAO objects, and Excel files. This testing approach can also be used with functional and unit testing.

99: How is database testing done?
Answer:
Database Testing is entirely based on the requirement specifications. There are a few things to consider related to database:
a) Default Correctness of data
b) Storage and/or Retrieval of data in database
c) The database is connected across multiple platforms
d) Indexing of database for better performance - Checking if the data insertion from the application into the database enforces restrictions on the data or not.
e) Data in the database is integrated
f) Security of the database

The in depth functionality aspects to look into being:
a) Checking for data constraints
b) Validation of the field size to see if it is correct.
c) The field size specifications in the application should match with the database field size.
d) Manually typing the query, to check if the table is providing the expected result.
e) Checking in Stored procedures
f) Checking for the insertion of data in two ways: One way is testing database from the backend, while inserting the values in the front end of the application. The second way is testing the front end of the application, while inserting the values in the backend of the database.
g) Database testing should check for performance,

functioning, and loading testing. It removes any data redundancy.

100: What is a Usecase? What is the attribute of Usecase?
Answer:
A use case is typically a list of steps, defined to interact between a role and a system and achieve a goal. It is an actor with a character. The actor can be an external system or a human. Therefore the definition of a Use Case is the explanation of the functionality of some features of an application in terms of actors, responsibilities and actions. Use cases are considered at a higher level to represent stakeholder missions or goals. It is a method used in system analysis and requirements in terms of identifying, organizing and clarifying accordingly. These requirements may be recorded as contractual statements or recorded in the System Modelling Language.
It consists of a group of elements say, classes and interfaces that can be used together rather than using the individual elements combined later. In this situation, there are greater results acquired by using groups of elements. The use case should contain all activities of the system that provide meaning to the users.
The attributes of Use case are:
a) Information about Document,
b) Description of requirements like functionality,
c) Objectives and goals,
d) Selecting the Actors,
e) Determine Preconditions and Post conditions,
f) Describe data elements,
g) Describe Primary flow (called a basic course of action), and exceptional flow (called an alternate course of action) of events.
h) Describe Business rules and implementation of interactions
i) Records paths from events triggered (these are called as scenarios)
j) Use case functionality of one can be used by another.

k) Use cases are used at several stages of software development, such as validating design, testing software, planning system requirements, and preparing a chart for online guide and user manuals.

Use case focused development is a key characteristic of software models. There are different frameworks such as UP (Unified Process), OUM (Oracle Unified Method), and RUP (Rational Unified Process) as process models. Due to this evolutionary and repetitious nature, use case is also used for agile process.

101: Explain an Emulator.
Answer:
A computer program (a system) or a device, that accepts inputs and provides outputs similar to that of a given original system is known as an Emulator. Further, an Emulator can be either hardware or software that replicates the functions of one computer system called as the guest, in another computer system called as a host. So, the emulated behavior thoroughly resembles the behavior of the real system. An emulator does not substitute testing on an actual device. An emulator is a hardware device in computers or it is a code that acts as if to be another program or a particular instrument that other components expect interaction. Usually, when a popular hardware device is outdated and no more exists in the market, legacy applications still exist and needs to communicate with the older hardware device. At this stage, an emulator is offered to complete the operation. This process of making an older program work with a new device is known as terminal emulation.

An example is a method of testing a mobile site by using a phone emulator. This is usually a desktop application or Web hosted application that imitates the device experience for a particular feature or group of devices. The accuracy between browser emulators and the phone varies. The browser emulators render a rough estimation.

Emulators are a useful tool for development to have a quick

verification check of code behavior without installing it on the real mobile browser. On another note, no matter how perfectly a browser imitates the rendering of a page on a real device; their overall experience cannot be reproduced as on a real device. This is due to factors such as latency and network speed involved. Therefore, though emulators are a very useful means in any testing process, they can never be used to replace real device testing.

102: Explain testing in web application architecture.
Answer:
Web application architecture consists of 3 phases for testing. This is also known as 3 tier application architecture.

   a)   Web tier testing
   b)   Middle tier testing
   c)   Database tier testing

Web tier testing – The first tier of the architecture is the web. In a Web tier application, it consists of a user workstation with programming that provides the graphical user interface (GUI), application specific entry forms and other interactive windows. This is the front end of the system and is a visible unit to the user. It is the first interactive phase for the user. Testing is done at this stage to check the browser compatibility for IE, Opera, Netscape, Firefox, and many more. GUI testing and cosmetic testing can also be done.

Middle tier testing -- This is the second or middle tier of the architecture. Major part of the functionality of the application is taken care at this stage. Mathematical, statistical, Business logic or scientific calculations and web based functionality is carried out and testing is done to check for proper functionality. Therefore functionality testing according to the requirement is done and Security testing can also be done.

Database tier testing – This is the third tier and is the back-end tier. Testing is done to check for database integrity and its contents. Database program is written to read and write data into it. Typically, email ID, contact information, library, reports and more vital information are stored in the database. All kinds of performance testing like Load testing, stress testing, reliability testing, and recovery testing can be done at this stage.

103: Explain VSS.
Answer:
VSS is Visual source safe and is also known as Virtual Source Safe. It's a configuration management tool or version control Tool (virtual library). After completion of coding of all phases of the development team, developers store the code in the development folder of VSS. Testing team copies code from that folder to testing folder, after completing testing for all phases; testers put the build version in the base folder. This tool is mainly useful to a developer, to store code and maintain versions.

In another instance, the activity involved here is, maintaining documents like Functionality requirements, Software requirement, Test Plan and more which is stored in a server. Any configurable item for a project is stored. A server is only accessible by administrator and VSS documents have read only permission and no modifying. All the clients' systems attach to this server and can access the documents with respective permissions.

   a) Developers can read and write documents with access (logins) provided to them.
   b) Testers can only view/read the documents with the access provided.
   c) Team lead also has access to view any updated file or document.

Generally, Development team can check in (upload modified documents to the server) and check out (download documents to their local system) while testers can only check out. This process is carried on throughout the life cycle. The below procedures completes the intention of the tool.

   a) Identifying the configurable items in the project
   b) Keeping them in a repository
   c) Maintaining version controlling.

This takes the complete form of VSS process.

104: What is backend testing using SQL?
Answer:
Checking the back end means, verifying proper database communication from the front end. It is to check if the database responds effectively to a query or statement executed. This shows if the data submitted by a GUI (front end web) program is updated in the database. This method also ensures the connectivity of database to that particular change or updates. This method of testing also checks to see if the changes directly made in the database are mirrored in the application. This shows that front end and back end, must be appropriately integrated.

Backend testing can also mean as server side testing. Servers are run on Unix - AIX or Solaris, mainframe systems and Linux. Below are the key aspects of the backend testing of a database or server side.

a) Data integrity test
b) Data validity test
c) A test to study the structure of the table
d) Functions, Procedures, and Triggers testing
e) Database performance test with Views and Indexes
f) Check Server logs
g) Check a Java based application logs
h) Check the Server response time and down time
i) Check batch processes and more

For example: A new column is added/created in the database table. Testing is done to ensure values entered from the front end web interface of an application are added and stored in the backend database.

105: What is Model based testing approach?
Answer:
Over a period of time with the popularization of models in software engineering and object orientation, there is an increase in black box testing methods. There are different methods of testing approach and these are collectively named as model based testing.

Model based testing (MBT) is a general term that indicates an approach with common testing tasks such as test case generation, execution and test result evaluation on the types of model of the application.

MBT is mostly used for applications in hardware testing. Particularly in telephone switches and a wide variety of software domains. Today, there are a number of software models in use, and a few make good models for testing. A particular choice of model based testing approach, may control testing as a success or a failure. Such model is used in software testing as a lead for test selection and verification. Such models are embedded in the application of testing by a tester with inputs in an adhoc method. Model testers help build encapsulation of application behavior. This allows testers to understand the application capacity and test it effectively with much possible range of behaviors.

These models based testers are written down (documented) and become sharable and reusable testing artifacts (use cases, test cases and more). Thus; testing here is known as model based testing. There are tester models, describing different characteristics of software behavior.

Examples are,

a) Data flow,
b) Control flow,
c) Program dependency graphs (Graphs that show implementation behavior by indicating its source code structure),
d) State machines and decision tables - Describes an external behavior called as black box behavior.
e) It is normal to think of MBT as, black box models by testing teams.

106: What is Migration testing?
Answer:
Migration testing is related to database. When data is moved from one database or databases to another, testing is carried on to ensure correctness and completeness of the task. The first database

which has the data is called as the source database and the second or latter to which data is to be transferred is called as the destination database. Database migration is done in two ways, manual and automation (through ETLs). In huge data transfers, automation through ETL (Extract-Transform-Load) is preferred. There are many reasons to transfer data.

a) Effective cost savings
b) Software and/or Hardware life cycle ends
c) Scalability and performance are to be enhanced
d) Minimize the risks (with existing product feasibility)
e) A consolidation and standardization plan is considered and completed on the technology front or standards front.
f) To accommodate changes in business structure due to the latest acquirement or merger completed.

ETLs (tool) are used to map data structures from old to new and may incorporate certain business rules to examine the data moved to the targeted database.

a) All the live entities (unexpired) (e.g. Customer records) are individually loaded only once into the target database
b) Process like data migration is performed faster without any bottleneck issues
c) Every attribute (in the source database) of every entity is uploaded into the target database
d) A particular entity with all data is uploaded in a particular relevant table into the target database

The following are test approach for migration testing.

a) Designing test validations
b) Setting up the test environment
c) Run validation tests
d) Report the bugs

107: Explain Migration testing approaches in detail.
Answer:
Migration testing involves the below procedures.

a) **Designing test validations**: SQL queries are hand written or using a tool. The queries are created to run and validate against both the source and the target database. The validation queries cover the scope outlined by the test requirements. The validation queries are arranged in a hierarchy based on the database relationships.
An example, 'Order Reports (records)' migration should be tested before 'Order Detail records', on the account that Order Details are logically dependent on Order Records. The test queries contain logging of statements for the effective analysis purpose. Bugs are reported after the tests are complete.

b) **Setting up the test environment**: The test environment is set up at this stage and contains a copy of database source, the ETL tool as applicable and a refined target database copy. The set up of the test environment is done in isolation such that any changes must not affect test execution.

c) **Run validation tests**: Depending on the test design, validation tests are carried out and the database migration process is not finished before running the tests.

d) **Report the bugs**: At this final stage, bugs are reported and an exterminated is called. Each failed test reports with the following information.
   i) Entity name that failed in the test
   ii) 'Number of rows' or 'Number of columns' that failed the test
   iii) The database error details (such as error number and description)
   iv) User account details under which the test was run and the time of the test that was run
   v) What was the validation query

108: How is portlet testing done?
Answer:
A portlet is an application (web based component with Java) used

to first collect or accept requests from clients and send information to the client by a portal website. Portlet testing is a workout to ascertain the quality of the portlet software. This testing is done on either local server or remote server by installing the application as required. Below are a few methods of portlet testing.

a) Test the size and alignment display with portal configurations and style sheets. Configuring a portlet object in the portal, must have the following alignments-

    i)   Narrow portlets (displayed in a narrow column side) with less than 255 pixels of width.

    ii) Wide portlets (displayed in the middle or a wide column side) with less than 500 pixels of width on the portal page.

b) Test all buttons and links within the portlet display. (In case of errors found, all forms and functions are verified for unique names provision).

c) Settings and preference changes are tested. (In case of errors found, the verification is done to ensure preferences are uniquely named and settings of the gateway are correctly configured in the web service portlet editor).

d) Secure information like a password, should use a tunnel tool to display and confirm that data is not stored in clear text.

e) Proper communication with the backend application is tested. Also checking for complete action's execution through the portlet is done correctly. (In case of errors found, the gateway is verified for correct configuration in the web service portlet editor).

f) Localized portlet should support all languages. (To make sure that the installation is done correctly for all languages and are accessible to the portlet).

g) Multiple versions of the portal are to be tested in case of backwards compatibility support.

This page is intentionally left blank

Testing Models or Process

109: What are different SDLC models and how is it necessary?
Answer:
A software or system process model is a description of the sequence of activities carried out in a Software Engineering (SE) project and the relative order of SE project activities. The SDLC model provides a generic fixed framework that can be tailored to a specific project. Project specific considerations for development will include:

a) Size, (years of completion of the software the number of people involved)
b) Budget, (cost or investment of the sources)
c) Duration (Time taken to complete the project)

There are different SDLC models to choose from for a business or commercial product.

a) (Test Driven Development)
b) FDD
c) Waterfall
d) Code and fix
e) DSDM (Dynamic Systems Development Method)
f) V Model
g) Spiral
h) Incremental or Iterative
i) Scrum
j) RAD (Reactive and Proactive)
k) RUP (Rational Unified Process)
l) XP (Extreme programming)
m) Lean
n) Unified process (UP)
o) Agile methods
p) COTS (Commercial Off The Self)
q) DDD (Domain Driven Design)
r) TDD (Feature Driven development)

Usually, a model covers the entire lifetime of a product. That is, beginning of a commercial idea towards ending of un-installation

of final release. Every model is based on three main phases:
   a) Designing
   b) Building
   c) Maintaining

Any model can be chosen for the development life cycle. It can also be changed to other methods, to improve below factors:
   a) Development time taken to market (speed)
   b) Visibility of the project
   c) Quality of the Product
   d) Involved Risk exposure (knowing risks better)
   e) Overhead Administrative factors
   f) Customer relations and more.

110: Explain Waterfall model and its use in SDLC.
Answer:
In software development, one of the earliest structured models is the waterfall model. It consists of the following chronological phases through which the development life cycle grows.
   a) **Feasibility of the System** -- In this first phase, the various targeted business aspects of the process are considered. The aspects that are necessary to incorporate into a system are found out. Finally, various methods to build the required software are determined.
   b) **Requirement analysis** – This is the second phase, where software requirements for the system are captured in a way that they can be transformed into actual use cases. These requirements, obtain performance goals, target deployment, use cases, and so on.
   c) **System design** - In this third phase, the system is made up of interacting components that is identified. The interface communication, the uncovered interfaces, input algorithms used, and the progression of interaction are all defined. The design and an architecture review at the end of this phase are conducted to make sure that the previously defined requirements are met.

d) **Coding and then unit testing** - In this fourth phase, code for the modules is written that make up the system. Review of the code is also done and the functionality of each module is individually tested.

e) **Integration and then system testing** - In this phase, all of the modules in the system are integrated and tested for all of the use cases by considering it as a sole system. This will ensure the requirements of the modules are met.

f) **Deployment and then maintenance** - In this last phase, the software system in the production environment is deployed. Errors are fixed that are identified in this phase. Additionally, functionality is modified based on the updated requirements.

The process involves development of the first stage and then it is tested. The process is sequential like a waterfall. Thus, the name of the model is known as the waterfall model.

111: What are the advantages and disadvantages of Waterfall model?

Answer:

Waterfall model has both advantages and disadvantages.

Advantages:

a) This model allows various phases of the life cycle to make into different compartments. This allows proper planning of the resources and gauge effort required through the development process.

b) Testing is enforced at every stage in the form of unit testing and reviews. There are stages of code reviews, design reviews, unit testing, and integration testing conducted in the life cycle.

c) In this method, expectations are set after each phase of deliverables.

Disadvantages:

a) There will be no completed working version of the software until later stage in the life cycle. For this reason, the system testing phase cannot detect problems at an early stage and testers have to wait until the application is ready for the test. Therefore, fixing defects is costlier in this phase than in the early life cycle.

b) It is difficult to change the design of an application during a testing phase, if these were not considered carefully during the system design phase. The prominence on early planning tends to restrict or delay the amount of changes that is initiated by the testing efforts. This is different from other models, which allows immediate feedback for development when the model is tested.

c) Every new phase can only begin when an old phase is completed. Such as, the system design phase will not begin until the requirements are finalized in the requirement analysis phase and are completed. Hence, this waterfall model cannot address uncertainties that may continue beyond the completion of a particular phase. This may lead to extended project schedules and delays.

112: What is Incremental model in SDLC?
Answer:
The incremental or an iterative model is a development model that splits the project into tiny portions. Each portion is queried to multiple iterations of the waterfall model. By the end of the iteration, a new module is completed or an existing module is enhanced. These modules are integrated to form the structure, and then the structure is tested as a whole. Testing begins at the end of the iterations.

For instance, a project can be split into 10 months (with one to four weeks) of iterations. Iterations of the system are tested at the end. The tested feedback is immediately included at the end of every test cycle. The time necessary for consecutive iterations can be reduced based on iteration's prior experience obtained. The system is developed by adding new functions of iterations during the development phase. Each cycle deals with a comparatively small set of requirements. Therefore, testing only evolves when the system grows. It delivers a sequence of releases to the customer/client as the iterations are developed and progressively functionality is added until the system is completely formed. In contrast to a waterfall life cycle each phase such as, requirement analysis, design of the system, and so on, occurs once in the entire system of the development cycle.

113: Explain advantages and disadvantages of Incremental model.
Answer:
Advantages of Incremental Model:
   a) This model allows taking corrective action immediately at the end of the iteration. Such as,
   b) The corrective actions can be taken for changes to the specification due to an incorrect interpretation of the requirements, or updates to the requirements, and other code related or design changes based on the system testing.
   c) This model helps to complete the project before the deadline, when there are less number of resources to work.
   d) Technical risks are well planned and managed.
   e) Core product with main functionality is developed first as an increment.
   f) There is faster delivery of product.
   g) Initial delivery cost is lowered.
Disadvantages of Incremental Model:
   a) Effective communication is very important for the project team, as it involves giving feedback about timelines, effort, deliverables, and so on.
   b) Requirements may continue to have changes in later iterations due to increase in customer demands. Therefore, it is tough to finalize on business requirements. When more iteration is added to cater the changes to the project, there are delays in delivery and cost exceeds.
   c) It is a challenge to have a very efficient control mechanism to manage changes made during iterations of the system.

d) Architecture of the project might face issues as a result of additional functionality added to the product.

e) Iteration of each phase is firm and does not overlap with each other.

114: Explain Agile model and its usage today. How is it advantageous?

Answer:

The life cycle of software development methodologies is mostly either iterative or follow a chronological model. In other words, this method neither follows a pure sequential nor a pure iterative model. As development becomes difficult, the models like RUP, Waterfall and V model, cannot efficiently adapt to numerous - continuous changes. Therefore, agile methodology is selectively a mixture of both development models. One of the principles of this methodology is fast and quick delivery. Hence the aim is to get accurate, practical and visible outputs in a short period of time. This method was standardized to respond to changes efficiently.

Agile methodology is a collection of principles, practices, and values that includes incremental development, testing, and suggestions or comments to form a new development style.

Agile methodology also has various approaches of development apart from Waterfall or Iterative methods. They are SCRUM, Dynamic Systems Development Method (DSDM), and Extreme Programming. Extreme Programming is the most extensively used approaches in agile method.

The key factor is having a continued customer interaction, and active participation of stakeholders throughout the development process until the delivery.

115: What is V model in SDLC?

Answer:

The V-model is another well known software model that represents a software development (or hardware development) process, which can be considered as an expansion of the waterfall model. Like the waterfall model moves down in a linear way, V

Model is bent upwards after the coding phase. This shape of the process steps is a typical V shape with development on the left side of V shape and testing phase on the right side of the V shape. The process execution happens in a chronological order in the V shape model. The horizontal axes represent project completeness or time taken and vertical axes represent level of abstraction. This model exhibits the relationships between each phase of the development life cycle and its associated parallel phase of testing. A parallel association of testing means, testing phase corresponds to each developmental stage. Meaning, testing is directly linked to each developmental stage. This is incredibly disciplined approach and next stage only starts after completion of every previous phase.

This model is also known as Verification (on left side – development stage) and Validation (on right side – testing phase) model.

116: Explain the V model with a graphical representation.
Answer:
Below is the graphical representation of the V model.

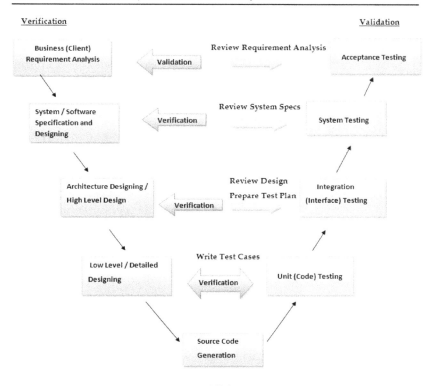

Installation

a) **Business Study and Requirement Analysis** -- This is the top most phases of the development cycle. The product requirement outlines the understanding collected from the customer point of view. There is a detailed communication (conversation) between the customer and stakeholders to know the expectations and exact delivery of the product. This is a very important aspect and requires proper management. This activity is crucial as customers sometimes are not sure about their needs. The design of acceptance test plan is prepared at this stage and business requirements are used as an input for acceptance testing.

b) **System Specification and Designing** -- When the user requirement is clear and product detailed requirements are derived, designing of the complete system is done. This stage is known as System designs. This would involve in understanding the need of the complete hardware settings and communication process setup, required of the product for development. Based on the system design, system test plan is developed. Preparing this test plan earlier, leaves more room for test execution later.

c) **Architectural Designing** -- This is also known as High Level Design (HLD). In this phase, Architecture is designed with the help of architectural development specifications. Normally, a couple of technical approaches are proposed. Based on the financial viability and technical advantages, the final decision of technical approach is made. System designing is further split into modules using different functionality.
The communication and data transfer between the internal modules and with the other systems is understood clearly and definitely. At this stage and information achieved, test plans are designed and integration tests are documented.

d) **Module Designing / Low level Designing** – This level is also known as Component designing and with as well other names. In this phase, the internal design is specified for all the system modules. The importance of the designing is to make compatible system architecture with the related modules and the other external systems.

e) **Unit testing** – Unit testing is also known as component testing, is a critical part of any development process. This helps remove the maximum faults, defects and errors at a very early stage. The internal module helps design the Unit tests.

f) **Source Code (program)**– Programs are written in this phase. Coding is the main and the basic phase of development of the system. This phase combines the two sides of the V Model.

117: What are advantages and disadvantages in V Model?
Answer:
Below are the V model pros and cons.
Advantages:
a) This model is a very good disciplined model and each phase is completed in a timely manner (one after the other).
b) Requirements are very well understood and therefore works fine with smaller projects.
c) The model is rigid and is easy to manage. Each phase consists of a review process and specific deliverables.
d) Easy to understand and apply and simple to use and manage
e) Most importantly, defects are identified at an early stage - User or Business Requirement analysis stage or System Analysis stage. Hence bugs or defects are fixed early
f) The Cost is less due to early defect repairs.

Disadvantages:
a) This model involves greater risk factors and uncertainty
b) This is not a good model for object oriented projects and complex projects
c) This is not suitable for those projects with fewer -unknown requirements and has a higher risk of changing
d) This model is not suitable for long and ongoing projects
e) Once a system or an application goes to the testing phase, it is difficult to go back and make a requested functionality change and this becomes expensive
f) Complete working software is not produced, until the last stage of testing in the life cycle

118: Explain Test Driven (TDD) Model approach.
Answer:
As the name suggests, Test driven is clearly led by testing methods in the first place. Test driven development model is one of the core exercises of Extreme Programming. This is the reverse model as compared to other traditional development process

models. The practice is an extension of the feedback approach. These involve that test cases are developed before the functional code is written or developed. The next stage is, developing of functionality by developers, to pass the written test cases. Once functionality is a pass, test team adds new test cases to the existing functionality. The whole test suite is run to ensure that the code fails. Here there are two types of failure to check. The failure may be due to the required functionality yet to be included or the existing functionality needs to be modified. The developers then amend the functionality or create new functionality in addition. So the earlier code should survive the failed test cases. This sequence continues until the functional program passes all the test cases written by the team. The developers then reason out any duplicate or lifeless codes of the functional code to remove it and make more maintainable. This is the approach to the Test driven development model.

119: Explain Test Driven (TDD) Model advantages and disadvantages.
Answer:
Like any other model TDD also has advantages and disadvantages.
Below are the advantages of TDD:
a) Because the functionality evolved is in small steps, test driven development promotes anxiously combined and highly reliable code. Therefore, the functionality of each code needs to be adequate enough, so that it is successfully tested in isolation.
b) The test suite is first created and this is a good input for functional specification documentation of the final system.
c) Due to test automation implementation, the time consumed for retesting the active functionality along with each new additional build of the system is significantly reduced.
d) Resolving the problem or a defect can be easily performed with clarity, when a test fails. If the test no longer fails,

then there is a clear measure of success. This ensures that the system meets the customer requirements.

Below are comparatively less disadvantages of TDD:

a) The fact that requirements are unclear. TDD relies on the feedback from both the customers and the developers for contribution on the requirements.

b) The Client or a customer or a representative is part of the team always and provides feedback about the functionality every time and this involves lots of additional communication which needs to be handled effectively.

c) The test suite has to be regularly maintained. Tests written are huge in number and are also code formation. Therefore, updating codes from time to time is tough.

d) Testing abstractions leak from time to time

120: Explain RAD approach.

Answer:

RAD means Rapid Application development. As the name suggests, this methodology implements a rapid development approach. This uses a component based production principle. A rapid prototype is created after studying the different requirements of the project with minimal planning. This prototype is then compared with the standards and output conditions as expected. Followed by the group discussion among the development team and the customer, required changes or modifications are made. This is a suitable approach for smaller projects.

There are different phases in the Rapid Application Development (RAD) model.

a) Creating Business model
b) Creating Data Model
c) Creating Process Model
d) Generating Application
e) Testing
f) Revenue generation

RAD approach is ideal to use when there is a system that requires modularization in around 3 months of time. It should be used if there's great availability of modelling designers and the budget is sufficient to cover both designers and code generating automated tool costs. RAD model is good to choose only if experienced business knowledge is available. When a short duration system needs to be produced, RAD is only then considered to be implemented as a model.

121: What are the advantages and disadvantages in RAD approach?

Answer:

Like other models, a RAD approach also has advantages and disadvantages

Below are the advantages of the RAD model:

a) This model helps and encourages feedback from a customer/client

b) It increases component reusability

c) Integration from very beginning solves a lot of integration issues.

d) Time taken for development is reduced

e) Reviews occur early and quickly

f) Software can be written faster and allows easy changes with requirement due to shortage of broad pre planning.

Below are the disadvantages of the RAD model:

a) This model requires individual performances and strong team building for identifying business needs

b) This model cannot be applied to cheaper projects as very high investment is required for automated generation of code and modelling

c) Only modularized system can be built using RAD

d) There is a great dependency on modelling skills

e) It requires extremely skilled designers and developers

f) It is suitable for small time projects with less changes in requirements

122: Explain Spiral Model approach in SDLC.
Answer:
This is another SDLC model of approach in IT for development projects. This model combines the characteristics of waterfall model and prototyping model.

The approach followed in the spiral model is considered with a number of cycles of chronological steps of the water fall model. The cyclic nature here is termed as Spiral. When the first cycle is completed, reviews of the product achievements are performed and a thorough analysis is done. If this cycle does not meet the expected standards and specified requirements, next cycle is followed and so on until the completed cycle meets the requirements. This is a similar method for iterative model approach, but suits for large projects with complexity and consistent change in requirements. Since it is used for large projects, the large expenses are also covered here.

Below are a few steps of the spiral model in detail.
a) A much detailed definition of the new system requirements is obtained by interviewing the key responsible people.
b) The new system will have an initial designing.
c) With the help of initial designing, the first prototype is constructed. This is normally a measured system to indicate rough calculation of the features of the final product.
d) A second prototype is developed by
    i)   Evaluating the first prototype's, strengths, risks and weaknesses
    ii) Defining and planning the second prototype requirements
    iii) Designing - Building - Testing, the second prototype
e) If the customer opts, abortion of the entire project is possible, if the risk is believed to be very high and low satisfaction of the project. Risk factors may be due to miscalculation of operating cost, flooded development costs, or any other factor.

f)   Prototypes are developed when previous cycle is not
     satisfied and process continues until a final product is
     evolving with customer satisfying results.
g)   A final desired product is developed by refining the
     prototype.
h)   The final system is meticulously tested and evaluated.
i)   Maintenance is carried out in routine to prevent failures
     on a large scale.

123: List the advantages and disadvantages of the Spiral model.
Answer:
Spiral model also has disadvantages apart from the advantages.
There are advantages of Spiral Model

a)   One of the most flexible models is Spiral model. A resolute
     is made by the project manager for a complex project
     about the development phases.
b)   The model is more transparent with each phase and each
     loop reviewed by concerned people. Thus, a project
     examining is effective and easy.
c)   Risk management is an inbuilt feature of the model and
     thus is opted compared to other models.
d)   Functional changes can be added at a later stage.
e)   The estimates of the project in terms of cost, schedule, etc.
     becomes even more rational as the project proceeds and
     loops in the spiral model get completed.
f)   Best suited for huge risk projects with unstable business
     needs.
g)   This Model helps build a highly customized product.
h)   Early stage software is produced

There are disadvantages of Spiral Model

a)   Huge investment (costly) is required for the project
     development.
b)   It has a complicated approach. It is tough to effectively
     employ protocols and rules in this model throughout the
     project.
c)   Need experienced and skilled resources. Project

evaluation and review should be done periodically.
d) Prototypes cannot be reused in other projects in future, due to various customizations endorsed by the client.
e) Low risk projects are not considered in this model.
f) Meeting schedules and budgets are tough requirements.
g) There is a great amount of documentation involved in transitional stages.
h) This makes complex management of the project.

124: Explain the RUP model approach in SDLC.
Answer:
RUP is another important SDLC model and is similar to Spiral model. Here, testing procedure on the whole, is divided into multiple processes (cycles). Each cycle has four stages
a) Inception
b) Elaboration
c) Construction
d) Transition

At the end of a first cycle, the product or output is reviewed and analyzed for any further cycles to be created. Another cycle is evolved with the above phases if the first output is not satisfactory. Then second cycle, third cycle and so on are created until final cycle is frozen upon complete requirement satisfaction. A slightly modified process is evolved from RUP model and is known as EUP (Enterprise Unified Process).
Testing team can carry out testing for all four responsibilities at any single time. But the roles and responsibilities must be clearly defined for artifacts and other activities. This allows the RUP testing discipline for a small scale business with a single tester to a large scale business with testing members, distributed across multiple continents.
RUP is not just a single solid regulatory process, but rather a malleable framework process. This is intended to be tailored by software teams on a project and the development organizations to select the fundamentals of the process that are suitable for their

needs.

125: Explain RUP model advantages and disadvantages.
Answer:
Advantages of RUP Model in SDLC:
 a) This model insists on a perfect documentation and is thus a complete methodology
 b) This approach can resolve risks proactively, when a client requires changes in requirement. Change request is carefully managed.
 c) System Integration involves less time throughout the model's development cycle.
 d) Due to reuse of components, time involved in development is less.

Disadvantages of RUP Model in SDLC:
 a) This Model requires experienced team members in their respective field to develop software.
 b) This is an extremely complex development process and is disorganized.
 c) Cutting edge projects use the latest technology; therefore re-use of components is not achievable. Hence saving time is impossible to fulfil even if it could be made.
 d) Integration through the project process is not a good activity with huge projects and multiple developments. This adds to the confusion and creates more issues at the testing stages.

126: Explain COTS model approach for software development.
Answer:
COTS can be expanded as Commercial Off the Shelf model. COTS are ready available built in software used to build other potential software. Most server side and desktop side software are COTS. They come with a wide range of options and characteristics that fit into all the challenging needs of adaptable customers. COTS products are put into operation by using built in configurations, which allow the functionality of the system to be specifically

adapted to customer needs. Reuse of software based on COTS has become very common. The majority of latest business information system's processes are built using COTS in place of object oriented system approach. Though there are problems using this approach, reuse of COTS still shows that it reduces the time taken to deploy the system and its efforts involved. COTS can either be used as software or hardware.

COTS are of two types, Solution system COTS and Integrated systems COTS.

Solution systems -COTS, consist of a basic application that is configured to customer needs from a particular vendor.

Integrated systems -COTS, involve combining more than one COTS systems.

These are the COTS approach in SDLC.

127: Where is COTS used?
Answer:
Cots are used in software and hardware and to build other software.

COTS used for Software:
  a) Operating Systems - OS2, UNIX and Windows/NT
  b) Graphics Packages - Motif and so on
  c) Databases – Sybase and Oracle

COTS use for Hardware:
  a) Peripherals - Keyboards, Monitors, Printers, and more.
  b) Processors - HP, Motorola, Intel, Sun
  c) Busses – cPCI, PCI, VME
  d) Disk Drives - Red Rock and Western Digital

COTS are used in various other applications.
  a) Integration solutions such as software frameworks, CORBA, Enterprise Java Beans, MS COM+, and more
  b) Third party vendors such as Java beans and component libraries
  c) Software engineering such as generic programming (polymorphism, etc.) and application generators.
  d) Finished packages for commercial such as spreadsheets,

databases, web browsers, word processors, etc.
- e) WSDL - Web Services Description Language
- f) SOAP - Simple Object Access Protocol
- g) Open source Interface designing like - ISO standards, XML, and more.
- h) UDDI - Universal Description, Discovery and Integration
- i) JINI - Java extension for discovery of service

128: Explain advantages and disadvantages in a COTS Model.
Answer:
Like any other model, COTS also have advantages and disadvantages.
Advantages:
- a) It provides fast and cheap solution
- b) Existing products can explore solutions with COTS
- c) All the basic functionality may be provided by COTS
- d) It is a distinctive integration project and is easy to execute
- e) Outsourcing can be done
- f) Build partnerships through planned supplier
- g) Easy execution into existing systems without any customization required
- h) This can be reasonable in cost and more reliable than any other custom software
- i) Requirements are determined largely by market research
- j) Often used by the business world instead of custom software
- k) Open markets can sell COTS

Disadvantages:
- a) COTS is more maintainable because the systems documentation is provided with the application
- b) The application can have higher quality only through competition, that improves the product quality
- c) COTS is of higher complexity because specialists within the industry have developed the software
- d) The marketplace drives the development of the application and not the industry

e) The delivery schedule is reduced because of the basic schedules involved in operations

f) It may have limited functionality or drifted requirements

g) Component identification due to mistakes, can be difficult

h) There are licensing issues such as shareware, freeware, etc.

i) There may be loss of control or compatibility issues

j) Specific needs of an organization might not be met

k) Market research is needed, which largely determines requirements.

129: Explain FDD model in SDLC.
Answer:
FDD is Feature driven design model in SDLC. It is an iterative or incremental software development method. It is one among agile methods for developing software. FDD approach is helpful to apply agile methods to greater projects and teams. FDD combines a number of best recognized industry practices, to become completely consistent. These practices are all determined from a client feature and value perspective. The FDD main purpose is to deliver concrete-working repeated software in a well-timed manner. Different challenges are presented by larger teams. This model calls for great attention to quality and is liked by all stakeholders in the process such as 'managers, customer, and programmers'. It has great reporting visibility, which allows developers to see quick information such as progress reports. It is built around best core industry recognized set of practices. It has five framework activities (feature driven) with customer appreciated processes. The first three processes are done at once and are planned for setting up the majority of the whole project. The remaining two processes are iterated over repeatedly, building up feature wise until the project is completed.

130: Explain advantages and disadvantages of the FDD model approach.
Answer:
Below are the advantages and disadvantages of the FDD model

approach

Advantages:

a) The five processes in practice helps in bringing new staff within a short ramp-up time.

b) An updated system is always ensured through a regular build. This can be demonstrated to the client. It also helps in early identifying of the errors in the integration of the source code for the features.

c) There is a visibility into results and progress of the project - This is achieved by appropriate, frequent and accurate progress reporting from within and outside all levels of the project. Reports are based on work completion; and these help managers at routing a project correctly.

d) Risks are reduced via design iteration & build in small lumps. This is possible through understanding, thorough system requirements and giving no room for uncertainty.

e) A high level walk-through of the scope and context of the project system is done. Later, domain walk-through is covered for each modelling area in a detailed manner.

f) Project's costs based on feature, leads to greater accuracy.

Disadvantages:

a) There is no written documentation.

b) This is used for larger projects and is not as powerful as smaller project, which involves one developer and only one person to model.

c) The project highly depends on chief programmer who acts as a lead designer, a mentor and a coordinator.

131: What is Scrum Model in SDLC?

Answer:

Scrum is an incremental software development, agile framework for managing application development or software projects. As opposed to a sequential traditional approach, its focus is on a flexible holistic product development strategy. The development team works as a single entity to reach a common goal. A self organizing multiple small teams is created in this model through working under one location and effective verbal communication, well trained, self managed and maintenance of discipline among team members in the project.

The principle of Scrum is that during a project, the clients can change their needs about what they want (called as requirements churn) which is recognized effectively. In such situations, scrum utilizes real time decision making methods based on information and actual events. Scrum adopts a practical approach and understands that the problem cannot be defined. Thereby, focusing on increasing the team's ability to quickly deliver and respond to rising needs.

Scrum is assisted by a Scrum Master, who is accountable for removing hindrance to deliver the goals of the product and deliverables at the ability of the team. The Scrum Master is a buffer between the team and any disturbing influences and not a project manager (or team lead). The Scrum Master makes sure that the Scrum process is applied as planned. The Scrum Master is the enforcer of the Scrum rules, conducts meetings, and confronts the team to improvise. The 'role' also refers as a leading servant to emphasize these double perspectives. The Scrum Master does not have any people management responsibilities.

132: Explain advantages and disadvantages of Scrum model.
Answer:
Scrum Advantages:
   a) It saves time and cost for the company.
   b) The Scrum methodology enables projects to be developed which is hard to measure.
   c) It is fast and allows cutting edge developments with quick coding. Testing identifies a mistake easily and rectifies.
   d) There are regular meetings, thus a clear visibility of the project development is found.
   e) This is also iterative in nature and requires continuous feedback from the user which helps being attentive to requirements changes.
   f) Individual productivity can be measured through daily

meetings. This results in the better productivity of every team member.

g) Issues are identified early and resolved early and quickly.

h) It is hassle free to deploy a quality product on time.

i) It works with any technology or programming language, but is effective for new media projects.

Scrum Disadvantages:

a) If there is no clear definition, it gets difficult to structure, plan and organize a project, by the Scrum master.

b) There is a regular product delivery, regular changes, and ambiguity regarding the exact nature of the finished product. This becomes an in-depth project life cycle for all those involved.

c) Furthermore, the regular reviews and daily meetings, require significant resources.

d) A project is successful only when the dedication and the maturity of all team members. It also depends on their ability to consistently maintain high level communication through each review and backlog.

e) Decision making is entirely in the hands of the teams.

f) There has to be constant, hands on management.

g) A task needs to be well defined. Else estimation of costs and time of the project will not have the accuracy. The task may occur with a number of sprints.

h) It is best suited for fast moving-small projects because it works well with undersized teams.

i) When a team member resigns the job during development, it causes a huge contrary effect on the project development.

133: What is XP Model approach in SDLC?
Answer:

Extreme Programming (XP) is a method of SDLC for software development. This is one of the most well-known agile software development methods. Extreme Programming also differs from traditional methodologies. It mostly provides significance to adapt rather than expectedness. XP accepts that requirements changes are ongoing - often a natural and unavoidable aspect of software projects.

This method believes that adapting to changing requirements at any point during the project life cycle is a more realistic approach and better than trying to define all the requirements at the start of a project. Later expanding the effort, to accommodate changes of the requirements is done. This system is more flexible when it comes to changes. The aim of XP is to reduce the cost involved in making changes.

XP advises a set of daily practices for developers and managers. These practices are aimed to represent and support particular values. Such an exercise extended to extreme levels, leads to a development process that is more approachable to customer needs and is called as the Agile development method.

134: Explain XP Model process in detail.
Answer:
XP is based on values such as Communication, feedback, Simplicity and courage. There are fundamentals of XP.

a) Unit testing is written before code programming and tests are run throughout the process.

b) Integration of components is done and testing is carried out for the entire system, numerous times in a day.

c) All software is produced in pairs with two developers sharing one screen.

d) A project initially starts with simple designing and evolves constantly to add flexibility during which, unwanted complexity is removed.

e) Production with smallest system is quickly put in place and then raising it.

The basic stages of XP activities are

a) Coding

b) Testing

c) Listening

d) Designing

Testing is carried out to ensure, all tests are passed, duplicate codes are removed and coding is very communicative. Types of testing generally carried out are, Functional testing and Unit testing.

135: Explain advantages and disadvantages of the XP Model process.
Answer:
There are advantages and disadvantages of XP model.
XP Advantages:
a) The chances are more that the system or product meets customer requirements confidently, since it is customer focused from the initial stage of coding.
b) The prominence of small - increment release reduces the risk on the project by enabling client/users to provide effective feedback.
c) There is continuous testing and integration testing increases the quality of a good work.
d) XP model and method is comfortable for programmers who do not like a typical software process.
e) Software efforts are better managed.
XP Disadvantages:
a) XP pays attention on a single team; project, development and maintenance.
b)   XP is typically vulnerable and requires well disciplined developers or programmers.
c) XP cannot work in an environment with a complete requirement, specification or design before programming begins as claimed by a client or manager.
d) Programmers cannot be working under different geographical environment.
e) Scalability issues of a system are not established under XP - new function (an application) must combine (integrate) to existing systems.

136: What is DSDM Model in SDLC?

Answer:

DSDM can be extended as a Dynamic systems development method. It is an agile project framework. DSDM is originally required, providing some order to the RAD (rapid application development) method. DSDM is a general approach to software project management and delivery of the solution. DSDM is an incremental and iterative method that holds agile development principles. This includes persistent user or client involvement. DSDM fix quality, time and cost at the onset and the scope is prioritized to meet the fixed time limit.

There are a few principles.

  a) The business needs focus
  b)   The project should deliver on time
  c) It has to collaborate
  d) Quality is never compromised
  e) Build incrementally with firm foundations
  f) It has iterative developments
  g) Communication should be continuous and clear
  h) Demonstrate good control of the overall project
  i) DSDM teams must be authorized to make decisions.

DSDM has instrumental factors which need to be met for it to be a success. If these factors cannot be met, it poses a risk to the approach.

137: Explain advantages and disadvantages of DSDM Model.

Answer:

These are **advantages** of DSDM model:

  a) It is crucial to have active user/client involvement. Users are likely to commit to the system and provide feedback. This helps reduce training costs.
  b) No decisions need to be verified as the team makes effective decisions themselves and this makes the development process more efficient.
  c) Delivery of products is visual and speedy in progress.

d) Business should suite the necessary criteria for deliverables acceptance and therefore it meets business objectives.
e) The initial design is continuously improved.
f) All changes are reversible and there unsatisfactory designs are removed.
g) Ensures most important requirements are met at a high level.
h) The integrity of the system is ensured.
i) The aim is catered by a mutual approach between all team members (stakeholders).

These are **disadvantages** of DSDM model:
a) It is costly to implement. DSDM needs both skilled developers and clients/users, and are trained to utilize the approach effectively. Therefore, it may not be applicable for one off projects or small projects or organizations.
b) It involves licensing cost.
c) It is comparatively a high obstacle for entry.
d) There needs to have an educational modification in the organization.

138: What is DDD Model in SDLC?
Answer:
DDD can be extended to 'domain driven design' model approach in SDLC. DDD is a group of patterns and principles that help developer skill object systems smartly. If applied properly, it can lead to software constructions called domain models.
Encapsulation of difficult business logic is carried out by these models, and this closes the gap between code and business reality. It has a few pre-requisites for the successful application.
a) The team of the project should have experience in Design or Object Oriented Programming.
b) It is not an insignificant domain.
c) The project should have access to domain experts.
d) There should be an iterative process in place.

This approach is used for complex needs by connecting the implementation to an evolving model. Below are the principles of DDD model.

a) The project's primary focus is placed on the core domain and its logic
b) Complex designs are based on the domain model
c) Initiating a resourceful collaboration between technical and domain experts. This is to refine an abstract model iteratively, that deal with particular domain issues
d) There are artifacts in DDD to create, retrieve and express domain models.

139: Explain advantages and disadvantages of DDD Model.
Answer:
There are advantages of this model:

a) The main advantages of all would be professional logic within a user oriented (domain specific) common language
b) Small applications get high productivity
c) Even less capable programmers can easily work with the application
d) New requirements can be easily fit in, if each screen has its logic and this makes it possible to quickly change the product
e) Quickly finding the root of a bug is possible by maintenance guys
f) The professional logic results in designing, faster analysis, and development processes.

There are disadvantages of this model:

a) Application's Integration is difficult unless through the database.
b) Behavior cannot be reused and there is no thought on business issues.
c) Falling short of abstractions, there is no possibilities of reasoning or performing iteration work.
d) There is too much complexity, especially if the application

development to the enterprise level and there is still Smart User Interface use.

e) Migration to any other design is not possible, except of substituting each application.

140: How to select a Model for a process?
Answer:
There are factors used to decide a perfect or suitable model (approach) for developing software projects. The projects include few thought process which helps in deciding an approach.

a) There should be a large methodology in place for a project
b) Does the customer or a management dictate a methodology?
c) There should be an approach that lends itself to one's project in a better way
d) Which approach is most comfortable for the team?

The process activities involved are Software specification, design, implementation, software validation and its evolution.

The models of software processes are not mutually exclusive and are mostly used together. The person who chooses a model and its processes to perform the tasks for that model is known as 'process architect'. Each model is evaluated to examine its strengths and weaknesses. Then the 'process architect' selects the model that is best suitable. The following considers some of the criteria for the list during assessment of the models.

a) How well does the model tolerate the risks that may encounter
b) To what extent does the organization's development, has admission to end users
c) The importance of knowing early functionality
d) How well are the known requirements defined
e) Anticipation of requirement changes in magnitude and frequency
f) Knowing the intricacy of the problem and probable solutions for candidates
g) Knowing the managerial capability of the organization

Testing Domains

141: What is a Desktop application testing?
Answer:
Desktop application can be found running on workstations and personal computers. Testing the desktop application focuses on a specific environment. Desktop applications work independently when compared to other applications just with an operator required. There are sufficient hardware resources, a set of functions and an application required for correct complete functional work. Testing for Desktop application is a challenge as mostly it is developed for certain type of environment. The environments to name a few are Windows, UNIX, Linux, and Mac OS. The interaction of the environment with other parameters is condensed to zero. For testing, there are several computers required with various configurations. A software engineer knows everything about the desktop application and has complete control over it. Testing faces maximum complexity through the intranets with the number of servers and clients being known. Complete testing of applications is broadly done with categories like Backend database, GUI, Functionality, and Load.

142: What is a Client server application and its testing?
Answer:
Client server application testing means testing of two different components. The application is loaded on the server machine while the GUI application (or with extension as .Exe) is loaded on different client machine. This is a type of network architecture. Client and server can be called as two nodes and therefore also known as two tier architecture. The client sends a request to the server anticipating for the appropriate response. The server does the process as per the request and sends back the result. This environment is mostly used in networks like an Intranet. Testing is broadly carried out in different types like, functionality, GUI on client and server side, client server interaction, Load, and backend.
There are also other testing types included in the test plan:
   a) **System testing**

b) **Regression testing** - Regression testing happens between builds and also occurs in post-production (between system releases). Each new version release is tested with three criteria
   i)   New errors evolved need to be resolved due to the fix of previous defects.
   ii) Errors in the new functionality have to be resolved.
   iii) Existing errors need to be resolved and previously fixed/resolved defects must not occur again.
c) **User acceptance testing**
d) **Performance testing with multiple users**

143: What is a Web application testing?
Answer:
Web application is slightly different and complex to test. This three tier architecture forms a whole system. It consists of a Browser, a Web server and a database server. The browser applications would be developed in XML, DHTML, HTML, JavaScript and more to access. Web server applications are developed with Advanced Java, VB script, Java script, Perl, PHP, JSP and more. Database server is developed using Oracle or SQL server or MY SQL, or Sybase and more.

Potential bugs are to be found out and fixed through testing web application. The test is done on different web browsers and OS platforms before the application code is moved into the production environment or is made live. Generally, the Web application is tested for compatibility of the browser and back end, operating system compatibility, static pages, error handling, Functionality test, System testing, GUI testing, Usability testing, system testing, security testing, Performance testing and load testing. These test types check for application security, the website functionality, and its capability to handle network traffic and test its access to help handicapped users along with regular users.

144: Explain detailed Web application testing.

Answer:

Below are the detailed testing types or methods involved.

a) **Functionality testing**

    i) **Testing every link on a web page to load correctly and completely and ensure there are no broken links. Checking links consist of** – 'Mailto' Links, Internal links, Outgoing links, and Anchor Links.

    ii) **Testing Forms** – filling of forms with personal contact details and more. Forms' submit button should work properly with appropriate message display. It should ensure proper loading of the form.

    iii) **Testing for Cookie settings** – by removing cache or expiry of cookies and deleting cookies.

    iv) **Testing business workflow** – Start to end business flow should have continuity and meaningful flow.

    v) **Testing HTML and CSS scripts** – codes or scripts should not show up on the user interface page. Web pages and browsers should interact well with each other.

b) **Compatibility testing** - The web application should display correctly across different machines/ devices and tests ensure this.

c) **Crowd testing** - Select a large number of people (crowd) to execute tests.

d) **Interface testing** - Web Server, Application, and Database Server.
Testing the system response with interlinked connections between the above three layers. If the interface is not getting established, an appropriate message should show up to the end user.

e) **Usability testing** - Site navigations should work accordingly, such as buttons, Links and Menus navigate to different pages easily, consistently and visibly.

f) **Database Testing** – This is a crucial component of the web application and testing must be done to stress must be laid thoroughly.

g) **Performance testing** – Website should work under all loads.

h) **Security testing** - E-commerce websites should ensure with proper - sensitive customer information details like credit cards and so on.

145: What is the difference between the Web application testing and Client Server testing?

Answer:

Client Server testing	Web application testing
This is a three tier architecture testing. This consists of Client system and Server system.	This is a two tier architecture testing. This consists of a Web server, Browser, and DB server.
Testing carried out to test intranet applications without any internet (browser or website) connection is an example for client- server application. For instance, the company places the firewall so the server and its information are not open to the outside world. In this way, the business work related to the company, is secured by way of not allowing outside people with access to the application.	Testing an application in the internet by using the browser is called as web application testing.
Limited number of people are allowed to use the installed application.	Such a network application is accessible by a large number of people around the world (WWW – World Wide Web).

Client Server testing	Web application testing
Testing involved here is for the LAN network application.	Testing is carried out in WAN application.
The test types performed here are: x Manual support testing x User interface testing x Functionality testing x Configuration testing x Compatibility testing x Intersystem testing	The tests types applicable are: x Functionality testing x User interface testing x Browser compatibility testing x Security testing x Load or stress testing x Data storage and volume testing x Interoperability testing or Inter-systems testing

146: What are Domains in testing?
Answer:
Domain is the knowledge of the business category or field with major functional features having subject matter specifications. Domain testing means a person who has technical testing skills and subject matter business knowledge. This is a requirement aspect preferred by the client to obtain easy, and effective testing results. The tester needs to have gathered domain knowledge or to be from the domain background of BFSI (banking, financial, services and insurance). Three skill categories are evaluated before hiring a software tester.

a) Domain knowledge
b) Testing skills
c) Technical knowledge or expertise

The various fields in domain tasting are healthcare, Telecom, Properties, insurance, Real Estate, banking, finance, IT and more. Some of the diverse edges of domain knowledge that can be found are,

a) Mobile application
b) Protocol
c) Network
d) VoIP applications
e) Wireless application
f) Banking applications

Usually testers with experience are preferred, as their expertise in a particular field adds more value to the project and its process. It is believed that a tester has a better understanding of key business features, processes and issues. Thus, a tester can quickly deliver the tested product or software system.

147: What skills are required for Domain testing?
Answer:
The knowledge about the subject area of a particular project and testing it is known as Domain testing. This particular knowledge belongs to various fields such as finance, banking, health, sales, telecom, Insurance, media, Advertising, Medical, Travel and more.

As a tester this is important because one should know the user requirements thoroughly in these fields. The knowledge widely involves Industrial or organizational working procedures, Infrastructures and Designations, Study of mathematics and its Calculations, Commerce Background with study of Accounts and Finance, study of Statistics, study of Chemicals and Biology, Business Communications and Marketing, Business Administration, Industrial Services, Government services, Brokerage and Share market, Food and Agriculture, Clothing and Accessories, Fashion, Real Estate and Construction and many more. Based on these categories, a software application-user friendly template, and workflow is designed. One can test enough of the application accordingly with user perspective scenarios being covered. There is core testing knowledge (skills) which are also required.

a) Hunting of Bugs

b) Testing
c) Technical
d) Domain knowledge
e) Automation
f) Ability to Work under pressure
g) Communication
h) Programming
i) Quick learning and implementation

148: What if you don't have enough domain knowledge?
Answer:
It is a company based decision while hiring an employee for
testing. If the project is highly sensitive and requires core
knowledge in that field, then priority is given to Domain testing
knowledge while hiring. An example is Banking or Healthcare.
On the other hand, if knowledge on domain testing is not given
prominence; one can be placed on any project and the company
can assign any work. In this case, one might need to quickly learn
the domain with as many concepts as possible. Leaning ways can
be through a senior, trainer, a colleague, user guide or manual,
visit the client/customer site, online study resources and material,
Involving in events addressed on such domain, check with
domain experts and so on. Factors for learning are,
a) Understanding the product from the customer point of
   view,
b) What are the use and purpose of the application, and
c) How does the client or customer use the application?

Usually, companies do provide training to testers before assigning
any specific domain job.
Domain knowledge is applied in every software testing lifecycle.
Domain knowledge and skills can be acquired in another way by
voluntarily checking open source (similar project software readily
available online for free) software or project relevant applications
available online. A few online sources available are financial
software or graphics software. This method of working on open

source projects helps gain practical experience with defects and bug reporting and retesting. The tests that can be tried are unit testing and exploratory testing in Open source.

149: Explain BFSI domain testing.
Answer:
BFSI means Banking, Financial Services and Insurance. This term BFSI is frequently used by IT or ITES or BPO or KPO Organizations referring to the services provided by them in banking, finance and Insurance domains. Core banking services include Retail, Corporate, Mobile, Money Transfer application, Net banking application, Customer service, accounting software, Private banking, and debit/ Visa/Master/ Credit card applications. Financial Services with commerce background include Mutual funds, Gateways Payment, Treasury software, capital market, trading, Loans like mortgage, house loans, personal; stocks and brokerage, etc. Insurance services cover life and after life policies. The BFSI applications are tested with many testing types depending on the application design and criteria.
   a) UI testing
   b) Functionality testing
   c) Security testing
   d) Load testing
   e) Stress testing

One should know the user requirements and in-depth working procedures for testing. Testing of application should be done accordingly to the subject matter expert.

150: Explain Search Engine domain testing.
Answer:
A Search Engine is the list of relevant topic information searched and displayed to the user. There is a dedicated server and they are Google, Bing, Yahoo and many more. These are called as Search Engines. Search engines are slightly different from one provider to the other with respect to features. They are typically a library,

storing loads of information on the internet at WWW. A search engine job is to list relevant web pages on the Internet asked by the user. To promote the business, a publisher would like to place ads on the search listed page; or use Ad-words (keywords) to show up his website on the first page of the search results; or either would want to place on top of the search listed pages. This job is managed as part of a search engine.

These search engines have an algorithm coded at the backend to fetch relevant topic information from internet as requested (typed) by the user on the web page. Useful and possible items on the search result list include the electronic tools or the source material. The electronic tool is a web site that can provide a dictionary. The resultant list page can also specify important information just as a book that can be evaluated by its title. Search engine depends on the type of query, to show relevant information or exact information. Therefore, knowledge of the English query typing may be an advantage for a user or a tester.

A tester must know the terminologies and functionalities of such a domain for analyzing purposes. The tester is then capable of effectively imitating the user-end actions. In this way, a tester performs complete testing.

151: Explain Healthcare domain testing.
Answer:
Health care is known from American term. Health care has several sectors and provide health services and products in order to improve overall and individual health care. This includes life sciences, health equipments and pharmaceuticals, biotechnology, and services. As per UNS (united nation standards), the 'health care' word means activities of the hospital, dental services, medical, chemists and other activities relevant t to human health. Healthcare product testing is very challenging, when compared to other domain products. This is due to its complexity in many things such as development, designing, and impact on the patient data, diagnosis results, and safety characteristics. Healthcare products have to obey for regulatory-safety standards such as

IHE, HL7, DICOM, and HIPAA and implement them. This proves to provide good competition in the market with the other vendor. In this way, test engineers are faced with multiple challenges and deliver high quality results to the client or customer.

Testing this domain needs more knowledge in the health department to test the application. The knowledge includes chemical names, drugs, instruments used, tools used, hygiene products, surgery equipments, operational tools, diagnosing tools, and many more. Testing skills required are System configurations, Application workflow, Environment setup, Installation, scenarios for clinical usage, standards used, regulations, domain tools, Clinical datasets or test data, safety and risks and more.

Specialized testing types include, hardware testing, Image quality checking, performance, interoperability, reliability, functionality and concurrency. On the whole testing should meet industry quality standards such as ISO, CMMI, and FDA. There may be a few ways to learn this domain, to deliver quality software system or as a fresher.

a) Visit Hospitals and talk to respective professionals and end users
b) Browse or search results on Web for more information
c) Meet and discuss with Domain Experts, Business analysts, and Application specialists
d) Read journals and clinical materials
e) Refer User manuals and requirement documents within the organization

152: Explain Retail domain testing.
Answer:
Buying and Selling of goods to the end users are named as 'Retail' and this business is known as Retail business.

The major retailer section has an intricate profile of modern application of IT technology with the integration of contrasting functionalities. The IT systems need to work with efficiency round the clock. They also need to ensure usability, security, availability and accessibility. Business Retailers constantly need to improve their application's performance, which facilitates across in developing, maintaining and taking advantage on their competitors.

The world for Retailers is constantly changing with market trends; globalization and thousands of customers. The main reason for these companies into the increasing in retail business is the demand of branded products and its purchasing power. During this period of transformation, retail systems business is becoming critical and is evolving to offer competitive benefits. They need experienced QA partner who can execute a fair quality check, with no scope for error. This requires established testing services that address the needs for better and new ways to develop alleviate expense risk and verify a broad range of end user situation. Testing solutions should have affluent domain expertise with sturdy technical skills and capabilities.

The types of testing which are important, are Operational Acceptance testing, localization testing, device testing, functional testing, and more. This entire process is known as Retail domain testing.

153: Explain E-commerce domain testing.
Answer:
Buying and selling of goods and its services on the internet (World Wide Web) is known as 'E-commerce'. The words 'E-Business' and 'E-commerce' are sometimes used compatibly. There are a few main aspects of online E-commerce.

   a) Retail selling on websites with online user products catalogs
   b) Demographic data usage through web contacts
   c) Electronic Data Interchange (EDI), businesses exchange of data
   d) Customers are reached through social networking, email and instant messenger
   e) Buying and selling from one business through another
   f) Maintaining security of business transactions

Many retailers employ and enclose e-commerce solutions. Hence, Quality Assurance verification of integrated solutions and components are imperative in this business. Online projects have to address quite a few challenges with -

a) **Performance**: Online transactions alter on a daily basis with a gradual increase over a period of time and especially during the shopping or holiday season.

b) **Security**: Retail websites must fulfil the regulations and protect their online shoppers from theft of identity.

c) **Usability**: Shoppers have certain goals. User's products must be complete and deliverable. Shopper exits or logs-out from E-commerce websites immediately, if the products in their shopping list are not found or the website is slow or has bugs.

Testing needs to ensure with higher scalability and availability as the user volumes and traffic grows. This will enhance the experience of online shopping. This whole process is known as E-commerce domain testing.

154: Explain Telecom domain testing.

Answer:

Telecom is Telecommunication and is an expression used for the process of electronically transmitting and exchanging of messages. The Telecom sector is growing at a larger speed and doubling its growth every year passing by. Mobile usage is increasing and there by various telecom network providers have grown. Out of the many new developments happening in this industry is the entrance of the 3G technology. Reliance, Tata, Idea, Vodafone, Airtel, MTNL, VSNL and more are all the public and private players entering into the foreign markets as well. There are two enormous fields in telecom testing.

a) BSS - Business support system (invoice generation, IVR's, call centres, and more)

b) OSS - Operations support system (cell towers, routers, switches, and more)

By testing in the above field one can become a domain expert in the respective telecom industry.

Products are connected to the public switched telephone network (PSTN) or a PBX (telecom switch). These products are tested with a simulator, telephone line, bulk call generator, or similar telecom test platform. One need to have knowledge about protocol, pockets, networking concepts, NMS / EMS, sockets, Perl and more which involve in telecom applications for testing purpose.

Below are the types of testing that can be used for testing

   a) Performance testing
   b) Functionality testing
   c) Stress and load testing
   d) Service Quality testing

155: Explain Wireless application testing.
Answer:
Wireless application is nothing but WAP, Wireless Access Protocol. This was initiated by Motorola, Nokia, Ericsson and others for defining a security requirement that allows accessing information through wireless devices, like pagers, mobiles, two way radios, communications and Smartphone.

Wireless technologies are used to build long array wireless networks by performing short array individual functions. There are some extremely critical wireless applications in terms of risk.

   a) Medical professionals use mobile applications for inspecting an EKG (electrocardiograph) chart
   b) There are other wireless technologies like pagers that diagnose medical data
   c) Scanners that are wireless help stores inventory level tracking.

A unique testing strategy that can be identified and documented is required by the wireless application regardless of the technology. Although wireless web can be slow to gain pace, other businesses will still try to build and deploy initiatives of many wireless types, to serve customers efficiently. The various wireless devices are, Bluetooth, XML, WML, WMLScript, Security protocols and more.

Considering the risks involved in wireless technology a testing strategy for wireless applications is planned. The major criteria to consider are:

a)   Wireless Application Types – M-Commerce, WAP, Workgroup personal productivity (WPP), Business system integration, and Entertainment
b)   Demographics and audiences – Age, Geography, and Web usability factors
c)   Use of Technologies
d)   Tools required or used
e)   Execution of Test Strategies

The type of application determines the type of tests to be used. Tests are done for validating the requirements, integration of transactions, and use cases. Testing types include platform portability, Regression tests, Performance Testing, Integration testing and load testing through the tools. In some testing situations, Simulators are also used involving real conditions and real people.

156: What is mobile application testing and strategies?
Answer:
Mobile application testing is a process of testing hand held telecommunication devices such as a mobile which has a software application developed in it. This testing is done to check its functionality, consistency and usability. Mobile applications are either installed in the device or can be installed from various platforms from a mobile software supplier. There is a phenomenal increase in mobile devices and its features in the last few years. More mobile applications are in demand with rapid technology growth. Therefore a variety of developments in this field are posing challenges in the testing phase.

A widespread mobile testing strategy is essential for deploying mobile applications to the market on time and within the budget.

These testing strategies include,

a) Selecting end (target) devices in an Optimized manner – mix of simulator and physical device testing on various models to maximize coverage of tests,

b) Network and device infrastructures – Wi-Fi networks testing and tools for network simulation testing to replicate cellular connections, and

c) An efficient combination of automated and manual testing tools

d) Types of testing- different types of testing required are performance, functional, compliance, security, reliability, and more

Mobile application testing may also require testing methods adapted.

157: What are the challenges involved in Mobile web application testing?

Answer:

A Mobile Web application is viewed by users all round the world. Whether single country users or single network, mobile web applications help to understand the dynamic global.

There are several challenges offered by the mobile web global nature. By understanding the nature of each challenge, diverse technology options can be explored to manage problems and diminish risk. Some ways to achieve this can be,

a) Coming up with the right solutions with an evaluation of the Pros and Cons

b) Determining the technology that best suits the testing requirements

c) Testing naturally in each of the options available

The mobile web application testing challenges include scripting, network, platforms and devices.

a) **Scripting** - The array of devices challenges executing the test script (Scripting). Every Device differs in input methods, display properties, keystrokes, and menu structure. Every device does not support the function of single script.

b) **Devices** - Devices have different hardware capabilities and differ in screen resolution (sizes) and input methods (touch, QWERTY, normal).

c) **Diverse Platforms (OS)**- There are different Operating Systems for the mobiles in the market with its own limitations. Foremost ones are IOS, Symbian, Android, BREWMP, BREW, BlackBerry and Windows Phone. Testing is a challenge for single application operating on the same OS or platform across several devices.

d) **Network** – There are hundreds of network operators. A few major operators are CDMA, GSM. Others use less common network standards like TD SCDMA and FOMA. A different network infrastructure kind is used by each network operator limiting the flow of information.

158: Explain Protocol testing.
Answer:
Protocol testing is a generic term and is used by communication industries for testing of diverse protocols in the domains of Switching, Routing, VoIP, Wireless, Telecom, Security and more. Companies of products like Nortel, Cisco, Alcatel, Huawei, Juniper and others have devices for networking like routers, modems, switches, firewalls and wireless access points. Different protocols are used to communicate with these devices. For instance, Cisco routers use OSPF, EIGRP and more to switch over routing information. Here testing of the protocol means checking whether an OSPF protocol and EIGRP protocol are working fine as outlined in the respective standards.

Communication protocols are called as Datacom protocol are terms used for the protocol working in networking domain. These are mentioned in IP stack or TCP and its chief purpose is for routing and exchanging information.

Usually protocol testing is done by connecting a 'device under test (DUT)' to other devices like switches or routers and configuring the protocol within. Later, checking of the packet structure of the packets sent by the devices, checking protocol algorithm, scalability, performance and more is done by using tools like Spirent, IxNetworks, Wireshark, and many more.

159: Explain Protocol conformance testing.
Answer:
The process of selecting each requirement in a systematic way from the standards document and testing to check if the device under test operates according to the specifications is known as the Protocol Conformance testing. For this testing, a sequence of particular function tests is created for each requirement, which results in many tests. To run the tests sequentially against the device under test is usually done through automation.
Computer networking protocols of Conformance testing are defined in ISO or others. Testing both the behavior and capabilities of an execution, and testing, observation against the requirements, in the appropriate global Standards is Conformance testing.
For instance, checking if the 'ping' command functions correctly is conformance testing. 'Ping' sends an ICMP (Internet control message protocol) echo request to a router or an operational host and this router or host should return a response of ICMP echo. The 'ping' command is also sent to a non operational or non-existent host or router, and then report back as 'ping: unknown host'. The latter will be a negative conformance test.

160: What is VoIP application testing?
Answer:
VoIP means **Voice over Internet Protocol**, which is a group of technologies and is a methodology for the delivery of voice communications (telephone calls) and multimedia sessions over Internet Protocol (IP) networks (computer networks). These IP networks are the Internet. VoIP converts analog signals of voice into packets of digital data. This supports real time, either way conversations transmission by using Internet Protocol (IP).

There are many commonly associated terms with VoIP they are IP, Internet telephony, telephony, voice over broadband (VoBB, IP communications, broadband phone service and broadband telephony.

VoIP is supported through ordinary telephone service providers, which use special adapters to connect to a computer network at home. A few VoIP operations are based on the technology standard.

VoIP presents a significant cost savings over traditional remote telephone calls. This technology offers a broad range of benefits,

a) Like management of single network in place of two,
b) Reduction of telecom costs,
c) The capacity to deploy a new generation of congregated applications, and
d) Provision for simplified services to remote locations.

Voice services cannot be compromised by any business. Revenue, reputation and relationships, all depends on the phone with dependability. Thus, every company must take steps to ensure that their joint VoIP network delivers best quality for call and continuous availability. For this reason a VoIP application testing with network test bed is set up.

161: Explain testing method for VoIP applications.
Answer:
A practical network test bed is setup for initial VoIP deployment and long term ownership. Basically, this test bed enables application developers, network managers, QA specialists and other IT department to examine and analyze the behavior of applications (network) in a lab environment. This environment precisely imitates conditions on the current or planned production network. All relevant attributes of the network are covered by this emulation. There are best practices to both VoIP initial deployment and VoIP ongoing management challenges for applying virtual test bed network technology.

a) Record conditions on the network to describe best,

average, and worst case scenarios

b) Run VoIP services in the testing lab under real world scenarios by using the virtual network

c) Call quality should be analyzed with technical metrics

d) Call quality should be validated by listening to live calls

e) Repeat tests as necessary to certify remedies of quality

f) Employ end users for acceptance testing of pre-deployment

g) The above best practices should be continued to apply over time as part of a recognized 'change management processes'.

162: Explain Cloud computing and its testing.
Answer:

Cloud computing is an expression used to describe an array of computing concepts that involve a large number of computers in computer networking. These are connected through a real time communication network such as the Internet. Cloud computing is a synonym for distributed computing over a network, meaning the ability to run an application or a program at a given point of time on many connected computers. Testing approach to software causes high cost in simulating user activity from various geographical locations. Thus, testing of load balancers and firewalls brings expenditure on software, hardware and their maintenance. Cloud testing becomes effective when there is disparity in client requirement of the deployment environment. It can also be opted in case of increase in the number of users involved in the application.

Cloud testing is a type of software testing in which cloud computing environments are used in web applications to simulate user traffic in the real world.

Load testing and performance testing is conducted on the applications. It also ensures scalability and stress testing under a broad variety of conditions. This testing generally involves supervising and reporting on conditions of practical (real world) user traffic and load balance for a range of simulated usage conditions. Companies like Trigent and IBM serve cloud testing. Companies practising testing are challenged by several struggles like meeting deadlines and limited test budget. In detail, there are a large number of test cases, no re-use or little use of tests and users' geographical distribution add to the challenges. Testing needs to ensure inside or outside or both sides of the data centre to provide good quality service and delivery. This problem is taken care by Cloud Testing.

This page is intentionally left blank

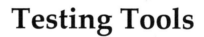

Testing Tools

163: Mention different tools in testing.

Answer:

The testing tools are divided into below categories.

a) **Test Management tool** - There are many Test management tools. These tools are used to store the information about testing to be done from the start to end of the process. Planning is done for testing activities and the status of activities of quality assurance is reported. The tools have a diverse set of features and thus have a different approach to testing. Normally they are used for maintenance and plan for manual testing; execute or gather resultant data from automated tests; multiple environmental management and to enter feedback about defects found. These tools provide the outlook of reforming the testing process and permit quick data analysis access, mutual tools and smooth communication across several project teams. These tools are capable of managing requirements to simplify test case design. There are many open source and licensed versions of Test management tools such as, Test Environment Toolkit (TET), Test Manager, TETware, RTH and more.

b) **Unit testing tools** – This is the process in which the least testable parts of an application, called components (units), are independent and individually dissected for proper operation. Unit testing is generally automated, apart from the manual way. Various tools are used for Unit testing. They are, JUnit, Rational Test, C++ Test, HTMLUnit, JsUnit, VectorCAST, PerlUnit, and many more.

c) **Functional Testing Tools** - This is a QA process where functions are tested by supplying them as input and examining the resultant output, and internal structure of the program is hardly considered. This process can also be automated. The combination of both open source and licensed tools available are, Rational Robot, Selenium, QTP, Sahi, QA Wizard, Test Complete, Soap Test, WebInject, WET, AppsWatch and more

d) **Load Testing Tools** - The process of putting force on a device or a system and calculating its response. There are automated tools to determine a system's behavior under both normal and peak conditions of load. It facilitates to identify the utmost capacity of operating an application and any blockage and identify the element that is causing degradation. There is also stress test done with the tools by raising the load beyond normal usage patterns. The Tools available are, LoadStorm, Loadrunner, Neoload, HP Loadrunner, Jmeter, Funkload, Winrunner, Forecast, Webload Professional and more.

164: Explain about the Load testing tool.

Answer:

The standard of a load testing tool is to replicate the performance of real users with 'practical' users. The tool then records the site's behavior under the load and gives data on the practical users' experiences.

The software is often distributive in nature. It is applied on numerous servers running concurrently, with each server replicating multiple virtual users. Most cases, the testing company builds up its own proprietary browser that can be shared by a set of instructions customized to each client testing business. The testing company manages by recording ongoing experiences of the virtual users' at the test site along with errors and response times. Companies also remotely monitor the client website to help diagnose problems with connection. The actual messages of errors may be recorded as experienced by the virtual users for later review. A set of logs is created and documented for each user experience. This information can be later judged with database testing information and CPU. This database testing information is provided by software testing team or testing tools provided by software companies.

This completes the load testing tool job.

165: Explain the functionality of JIRA tool.

Answer:

JIRA is a tool used for issue tracking, defect/bug tracking and management of the project. JIRA is software commercial product that has license for running on location or accessible as a hosted application. JIRA is coded in Java language and uses the entity engine called Apache OFBiz, the control container called the Pico inversion, and technology stack, WebWork1. JIRA also supports XML- RPC, REST and SOAP for RPC (Remote Procedure Calls). There is integration of JIRA with source control programs like CVS, Subversion, Clearcase, Git, Team Foundation Server, Perforce and Mercurial. It ships with various translations including English, Japanese, German, French, and Spanish. There is flexibility found in JIRA with plug in architecture produced at the large number of integrations developed by the third parties and community of JIRA. The API (application programming interface) of JIRA allows integration of application of a third party into JIRA by the developers. There are many release versions of JIRA, JIRA 1, JIRA 2, JIRA 3, JIRA 4, JIRA 5, and JIRA 6.

166: What are the requirements of JIRA?

Answer:

JIRA can be used as the test case manager with the following requirements.

a) Defining test cases before executing them.

b) Changing definitions of test cases for diverse branches and releases can be done in parallel.

c) Several tests executed over a period of time for a particular release should contain reports with information.

d) The outcomes of executing the test cases have to be gathered in some place.

e) Updating of the reports should be done easily, when the primary information changes. For example, when partial tests pass and fail, or old tests are removed and new are added.

f) Each release should contain the reports with a clear summary of the progress of the testing activities.

g) The reports' format should be in a way to archive assortment of self contained files like test logs.

h) There should be an automatic import into the test case manager, if a huge number of test cases are already defined.

167: Explain the functionality of Bugzilla tool.
Answer:
Bugzilla is a bug tracking system. It is a well known tool among developers and testers, which is free to use. It is an easy to use tracking tool. Bugzilla has a web based interface and can be easily configured for external and internal access. Bugzilla back end connects into a database to query bugs, manage, and store them. Normally, this database is also hosted on the web server.

Customers expect their deliverables to perform as expected. Tracking and resolving bugs is an essential process that heavily affects the quality of the product, productivity of the developer, and customer satisfaction.

It is a natural part for bugs to occur in the development process of the product. Usually in the development process, proper management of the bugs is the key to success and below issues need to be avoided.

a) A reported bug is never followed up.

b) Lesser priority bug is fixed before higher prioritized bugs.

c) A bug posted as a note, gets lost.

d) Recurring of bugs occurs, but no documentation to know how it was fixed in the first occurrence.

e) The developer's wrong assumptions of someone else fixing the bug.

f) Unable to reproduce a bug by the developer

g) Poor or un-clear bug reproduction by the tester

Tracking the life cycle of a bug can prevent problems with bug management. Thus, bug management ensures accountability, improves communication, and increases productivity. It provides team with high quality products, productivity and content customers.

168: Explain the features of Bugzilla tool.
Answer:
Bugzilla is a complete featured bug reporting system. It executes efficiently and quickly. The list of features is quite wide, but there are key aspects that make it a powerful tool.

a) **Bug Resolution logical Process** - This is streamlined through confirmation of bug, assigned, declaration and verification.

b) **View of Bug Dependency** - The result of a new bug depends on the declaration of a previous bug. Bugzilla supports dependencies of resolution and allows examining where the bug is held.

c) **Tracking Time** – Tracking is done to check the time spent for fixing a bug, and calculating against the original time estimation.

d) **Notifications of Emails** - Emails alerts are sent for any changes. Configuring an email can be done.

e) **Client Input** – client or customers can also access Bugzilla to track and choose the most desirable tickets to be fixed first. This helps to set bug priorities.

f) **Limited Access** - Authorizing access to either a group of engineers or to a single ticket.

g) **Three dimensional reports** – Configuration of reports is possible in three dimensions. Reports may be generated to show filed bugs, fixed and outstanding bugs. This is helpful in tracking the status and helping a project manager to allocate resources properly.

h) **Searches are saved** – Searching of Bug for future reference can be saved and is easy. Search is possible in any combination of features.
   i)   Operating System
   ii) Keywords typed in Ticket Text box

iii) Platform

iv) Severity of Bug

v) Priority of bug

vi) Version of the Software

vii) Assigned Developer/Engineer

viii) Software Component

ix) Email Address of the developer

x) Date of bug raised

xi) Wildcards and substrings

i) **Attachments of Ticket** - Attachments for additional information about defects or bugs can be added to a ticket. Example, input data on the occurrence of an error.

169: How does the Bugzilla tool function?

Answer:

When new bugs are noticed, they are created in the Bugzilla tool and then they proceed through a series of conditions, based on the call for actions made by the clients or developer. Each change of state can be documented within bug record for the data that can be reported or reviewed at a later stage. This history will make sure that issues are not forgotten. Below are the steps involved in the functioning of the Bugzilla tool.

a) New bugs are entered.

b)   Then they are set to the status as 'Assigned or Resolved'.

c) Bugs 'Assigned' are either 'Resolved' and closed or changed with the ownership.

d) 'Resolved' bugs can be Verified, Closed, or Reopened.

e) The developer takes control of a 'Reopened' bug, checks for confirmation and fixes it again as 'Resolved'.

f) 'Verified' bugs can also be 'Reopened', 'Unconfirmed', or 'Closed'.

g) 'Closed' bugs can be 'Reopened' or 'Unconfirmed'.

h) 'Unconfirmed' bugs may be confirmed as a 'New bug or Assigned or Resolved'.

A 'Reopened' bug may mean that it is not fixed; 'Unconfirmed' means bug is irregular or hard to trigger the case; and 'Closed' means bug is fixed.

170: Explain the functionality of SoapUI.
Answer:
SoapUI is a complete open source automated functional testing solution with cross platform. It is free to use. It has an easy-powerful graphical user interface, and class enterprise features. It is a web service application for SOA (Service oriented architectures). SoapUI allows rapid and easy creation and carries out automated test types such as functional, compliance, regression, and load. For an individual test environment, the tool provides a complete test coverage supporting leading technologies and all the standard protocols.

The industry technologies and standards involved are SOAP and REST based Web services, Internet Rich Applications, databases, and more. The test drive in SoapUI begins by creating a Project and then executing the test types. For a superior degree of automation, the tool also offers a set of command line tools that execute functional or load Tests and Mock Services. All this can be used right from any task scheduler or build process in an integrated part. There is also an option for scripting.

The key functionality covered by SoapUI is a web service inspection, development, invoking, and mocking. Using SoapUI, even the most advanced test scenarios can be created. It has an efficient Navigator on the left side of the main window which makes the progress and test organization always viewable. On the Project window, the entire project can be managed and controlled.

171: What is a Configuration management tool?
Answer:
A superior configuration management is crucial for controlling testing. Due to the nature of the software development life cycle, there are many builds and versions released. Each release version has some tests executed and respective bugs are discovered and fixed. Tracking these test case execution and their bugs is very important. It is important to know what exactly is supposed to be

tested, with respect to the exact version that belong in a system and expect bugs. Although these versions and test cases can be manually tracked, a tool like Configuration management can make things easier during complex environments. A Testware (a subset of software for testing automation) needs to be located under configuration management tool. The Testware also has diverse versions and is changed early or later in the automation life cycle. Characteristics of configuration management tools can be as,

   a) Storing information about the build and versions of the Testware and software.
   b) Traceability between Testware and Software and different variants.
   c) Tracking of versions belonging to configurations (OS, browsers, libraries).
   d) Management of a build and release versions.
   e) Base lining such as all the configuration items for a release.
   f) Access control such as, checking in and out.

172: What is TestLink?
Answer:
TestLink is a test management system of a web base that facilitates quality software assurance. It is built with MySQL, PHP and many other tools. The platform offers support for test cases, test plans, test suites, user management, and test projects, along with various statistics and reports. It streamlines the development process and enables testing teams to manage better test case execution and reporting.

The TestLink needs an administrator to access a web server and a database, to install and execute it. To use a TestLink, only a web browser is required by the user. The TestLink has many features apart from the below.

   a) Management of Requirements - Defining requirements and updating the changes constantly to ensure correct version.
   b) Specification of Test - Test Cases are defined by assigning

      into various Test Suites.

c) Assignment of Test Execution - Test Case execution is assigned at Build Level.

d) Execution of Test - Test Cases executed for identifiable Platforms, Test Plans and Builds.

e) Metrics, Test Reports, Test Execution Monitoring, Charts, and more.

f) It has centralized User and management of Roles.

g) Extremely customizable due to user defined Custom Fields.

Project Management in Testing

173: What is a code coverage tool?

Answer:

Code coverage tool evaluates the comprehensiveness of a test suite that was created using a method, along with the black box testing. This coverage tool allows examination of parts of a system that are hardly ever tested and makes sure that the most important functional points are tested by the team. As software metric, code coverage can be reported in the form of a percentage.

a) **Function coverage** - Execution of functions are reported in this coverage.

b) **Statement coverage** – Statement means the number of lines executed and reported to complete the test.

Cent percent statement coverage ensures that all branches (control flow) or code paths are at least executed at once. This method, does not cover enough functionality, but ensures correctness because the same code, processes different inputs incorrectly or correctly. Below are the different code coverage tools.

a) Debugger
b) Compiler
c) Profiler
d) Build automation
e) Modelling
f) GUI (graphical user interface) designer
g) IDE

174: What can be the general causes of bugs in software?

Answer:

Bugs can be formed in software due to ignorance. The factors of ignorance can be from technical leads or developers or managers or the top most person of the managing hierarchy. These are human factors for occurrence of bugs in software. There are general and technical factors contributing to bugs.

a) Development time schedule is unrealistic and is pressurising

b) Requirements are miss-communicated and this introduces

error in code
c) Lack of designing experience or poor designing
d) Human factors initiates errors in code
e) Lack of coding practices and experience
f) Lack of interest in learning new technology
g) Deficient of version control
h) Complexity in Software
i) Introduces error because of last minute changes in the requirement
j) Third party tools used have bugs
k) Poor Software testing skills
l) Poor technology knowledge
m) No coordination among developers
n) Developers do not look outside the company
o) Developers have limitation from going out and exploring stuffs
p) The value of developer tools is not known
q) Using Obsolete automation scripts without its update
r) Lack of skilled and domain expertise testers

175: What are technical types of bugs?
Answer:
Bugs occur due to various factors and they are a few types. One type of bug is due to permanent design faults and is mostly deterministic in nature. These can be easily identified and dug out during the testing and debugging phase or at an early deployment phase in the software life cycle. The other type belongs to the temporary interior faults class and is intermittent. They are basically permanent faults, whose launching conditions occur rarely or are not easily reproducible. Therefore, these faults are known as transient failures, which may not recur if the software is restarted. Some examples are boundaries between various software components, insufficient or improper exception handling and mutually dependent timing of various events. Below are the other types of bugs that are caused.
a) Inappropriate escaping of encoding or output

b) Inappropriate input validation
c) SQL query injection
d) Conditions of race
e) Scripting in cross site
f) Error messages with information leakage
g) Memory leakage
h) Error during sensitive information transmission
i) External control of file paths and critical data
j) Inappropriate initialization
k) Inappropriate authorization
l) Security checks at Client side

176: What are types of faults?
Answer:
A Fault is the incorrect state of software or hardware resulting from design flaw, physical defect, or operator errors. Faults occur during various stages or situations. Faults are introduced during system designing, during manufacturing and during operation.

a) Incorrect design in floating point division
b) Infinite loop is caused due to Bug in software
c) Bad or Poor solder connection between motherboard and chip pin
d) Broken wire within chip
e) Charge from Cosmic ray knocks off DRAM cell
f) Incorrect installation of new software by System administrator
g) Logic of Arithmetic is wrong
h) Fault in Code reviews
i) Multithreading programme fault
j) Fault due to Performance bugs
k) Algorithmic fault
l) Wrong syntax or typos mistake in Compiler
m) Precision and Computation fault - Not enough accuracy
n) Documentation fault - Misleading documentation
o) Overload or Stress fault - Maximum load violated
p) Boundary or Capacity fault - Boundary cases are usually

special cases

q) Coordination or Timing fault - Synchronization issues
    Very hard to replicate

r) Performance or Throughput fault - System performs
    below expectations

s) Recovery fault - System restarted from abnormal state

t) Hardware and software system fault - Compatibility
    issues, cosmetic problems, fonts, tab sequences, short keys,
    system / DB crash, integration failure, and more

u) Procedures and Standards fault - Makes for difficult
    maintenance

177: What is a segmentation fault?

Answer:

When a program tries to access a part of memory that is
inaccessible, or tries to access the program that is prohibited from
accessing is known as 'Segmentation fault'. This is also known as
'segfault or SIGSEGV'. This fault in the application is caused by a
bug. In technical terms, it means that applications try to read or
write to a part of memory that does not belong to it nor exist. It is
forbidden to read or write information to somebody else's
memory and when kernel of the system detects this, the
application is forced to quit. They occur in an OS like UNIX or
also in Windows, called as 'general protection fault' or 'access
violation'. It is a kind of program crash, and is an unusual
termination of a program.

Otherwise, Segmentation faults have various causes, commonly
found in C programming language, chiefly due to errors in
pointers for virtual memory addressing, mainly illegal access.
Another type of memory access error is a 'bus error', due to
misaligned memory access, or incorrect physical memory
addressing which is very rare. These are references of memory
which cannot be addressed by the hardware. Most or all of the
Segmentation faults happen from the same application. It is
possible to detect a bug only with proper and complete
information of the setup – environment – features used and

system on the whole. The 'error message' is the key to find the place from where it is occurring, and other messages if any. This is Segmentation fault and its various causes.

178: How is testing done in Software Project management?
Answer:
During or before the development of the software, testing documentation of artifacts should be developed for testing of Software. Therefore, Software testing documentation helps in estimating the efforts for testing required, such as requirement tracking or tracing, test coverage, etc. There is description of some commonly used documented artifacts related to testing, and the different phases of testing are,

a) **Test Plan** - It is a document that contains information on the project Scope, such as approach, testing activities schedule, manpower required, Issues of Risk, selected features to be tested, Environment Requirements and Testing Tools.

b) **Test Strategy** - It is a document arranged by the Quality Assurance Department, to attain the standards with the testing approach details.

c) **Test Scenario** - This is prepared based on the test scripts and test cases with a series of execution.

d) **Test Case** - It is a document usually written by the tester with the series of testing steps with respect to the behavior of functionality/ feature/non-functionality of the application. The Test Case document consists of ID, Name, Conditions (Pre and Post) or Actions, Expected Results, Environment, Actual Results, Pass or Fail headers. The Test cases can be classified broadly as Positive Test cases, User Interface Test cases, and Negative Test cases.

e) **Traceability Matrix** - This matrix establishes a way to make sure there are checks placed on the coverage aspect. It helps in creating a print to identify coverage gaps.

f) **Test Script** - It is a program written to examine the application's functionality. It is a set of readable system instructions and automated for easily performing regression and repeatable testing.

g) **Test Environment** - The testing is going to be performed in the Software and Hardware Environment. It explains if the software under test cooperates with Stubs and Drivers.

h) **Test Procedure** – It is a document that contains the detailed step by step instructions for one or more test cases execution. It is used in Test Scripts and Test Scenario.

i) **Test Log** - The log contains the output details (information) of test case execution details.

All the above steps are carried out in order as part of the software testing project management.

179: Explain Test strategy in detail.
Answer:
A Test strategy is a high level document which is normally developed by a manager and mainly defines the objectives for the approach in software testing. This is derived from business requirement specification document. The test strategy is the planning on how to advance in testing.

A test strategy provides a testing perspective on the whole, and identifies risks or references project requirements and plans. The test strategy purpose includes,

a) To obtain agreement of objectives and goals from stakeholders such as management, testers, developers, users and customers

b) Expectations to be managed right from the beginning

c) To ensure planning is carried on in the right direction

d) To categorize the test types to be conducted at all test levels

e) Relevant policies, regulations, or directives

f) Required standards, processes, and templates

g) Supporting guidelines

h) Objectives of Stakeholders and their tests

i) Test estimates and resources

j) Testing phases and levels

k) Testing environment
l) Criteria of completion for each phase
m) Required review methods and test documentation

180: Explain a bug life cycle.
Answer:
A 'bug life cycle' is also known as defect life cycle. The management of the bug in an effective way to have an error free software system, is the purpose of a bug life cycle. A bug life cycle often uses the tool to record the activities and stages of testing. The life of bug, means the time from when it is born or detected and fixed and then closed, is all recorded via the tool and this process is rightly called as 'Bug life cycle'. The bug reaches different stages in the life cycle. Below are the different states of a bug.

a) New
b) Open
c) Assign
d) Test
e) Verified
f) Deferred/Overdue/Postponed
g) Re-opened
h) Duplicate
i) Rejected
j) Closed

The tester finds a bug during the testing process and execution of test cases. This bug is reported to the test lead and after verification of the bug for validity; it is reported to the development team if it is valid, or else it is rejected. This is a 'new' bug and the developer head checks for validity and requires clear steps for the same. Now the status of bug is 'Open'. A developer is 'assigned' to fix the bug, after the bug is fixed; it is assigned back to the testing team with status set as 'Fixed'. Once the bug is retested, if it passes, it is marked as resolved and 'closed'. In some situations, the bug might be kept on 'hold' from resolving based on criteria like priority and severity from the release point of view or time constraints or client or user priority. At this point, the bug status is 'deferred'. If the bug is not considered by development team, the status is set to 'Rejected'. A closed bug may reoccur during the release versions development and the status is set as 'Re-opened'. Tools used for bug life cycle tracking have status naming convention slightly different from each other.

181: What is a bug management?
Answer:
Bug management covers more than just bug tracking, and there are many wide industry standards followed. The below job is easily carried out by the Bug management system during,
   a) Proposed changes to software
   b) Bugs and enhancement requests
   c) Complete or all releases

Bug management is done by tracking and managing through software programs such as Pivotal Tracker, Bugzilla, Trac and many more. These programs can track any type of change, and are called as tickets or issues as followed by the new agile development theory. Each issue is tracked by some type of categorization. These categories may be subjective or objective, a combination, such as severity and priority, area of the software, version number, and issue type (a bug or a feature request). Bug management has two types of reporting, one is known issues to fix and the other is issues that are on hold due to some reason. Bug management helps measure the bugs during testing that can provide an estimation of the number of possible bugs that is remaining. This becomes reliable, the more the product is tested and developed. The known issues can be fixed. The second kind of issue is informed to users that cannot be fixed in the existing release, or not fixed at all, or a workaround is provided. In such a case of bugs, 'Severity' tag is used to categorize the indication or definite behavior of the bug. 'Severity' levels are decided by software manufacturer and are not standardized. For instance, bug severity levels of the system might be,

- a) **A hang / crash**
- b) **No workaround** - The user cannot complete a given task
- c) **Has a workaround** -The user can recover and achieve the task
- d) **Visual or UI defect** - a missing image or displaced form element or button, or documentation error

Other manufacturers use skilled 'Severities', such as low, critical, trivial, high, or blocker. The severity of a bug is fixed based on its priority and the two are calculated and separately managed. These are the processes of a bug management.

182: How to achieve good test cases or what are the thumb rules to write good test cases?
Answer:
Every tester's job is to basically write test cases. Review of test cases is done and many times the reviewer rejects the test cases because of poor quality. A tester should know the characteristics of a good test case in order to write them. This is possible through many factors such as domain knowledge, testing skills, technical skills, experience and more. The characteristics for writing a good test case should,

- a) Be precise and to check only as intended.
- b) Avoid unnecessary steps in test case.
- c) Be to reuse test case.
- d) Be requirements traceable.
- e) Be regulations complaint.
- f) Be independent to execute it in any order without other test cases dependency.
- g) Be clear and simple, so another tester can understand it.

A few tips to keep in mind as a tester is,

- a) To make sure the test case tests only one thing and not multiple conditions in one test case. Otherwise, it becomes extremely tough to track results and errors.

b) Consistently organizing the test cases in many ways by following the same patterns.

c) Writing small test cases by mentioning its purpose adequately and clearly, for each test case.

183: What is the Scope of testing?
Answer:
Projects expand on a system and make it impossible to accomplish deadlines. This creeping nature of the system needs to be controlled and is necessary to define the capacity at the very beginning based on the Business Requirements Analysis of a project. This is then managed closely against the 'signed off' description. This process is called as the Scope of testing and other activities may involve Scope control.

A properly defined scope will have a clear understanding about testing to be carried out.

Information on what features to be tested and not be tested has to be understood. It is vital to know areas of team responsibilities and what types of testing are required for the product such as Security, Performance, globalization and more. 'Scope of test' in brief illustrates the resources of the test plan, such as responsibility, phases and risk factors. Therefore, defining the scope for testing a project is very essential for the management.

184: What are the 'Defect Density' and its uses?
Answer:
The Defect Density can be defined as the detected number of definite defects in a component or software during a distinct period of operation or development against the software or component size.

In other words, Defect Density is a calculation of the total defects known divided by the software body size Also Defects per KLOC (per one thousand line of code) are calculated as Defect Density. The Formula can be written as: Defect Density (period) = [Number. of. Known Defects / Size]
Here,

   a) The defects are agreed upon and confirmed apart from being reported.

   b) Defects that are 'dropped' are not considered.

The time (period) might be considered for any of the following,

   a) Duration, such as the first month, or quarterly, or the whole year.

   b) Each stage of the software life cycle.

   c) The entire life cycle of the software.

The size is calculated in one of the following ways:

   a) Coding Source Lines

   b) Functional Points - FP

Where, 'The Number of Known Defects' are the total defects' count, identified against particular software entity, during a particular time period. Size allows comparisons between different software entities, like releases, modules, products and it normalizes.

185: What are a Defect Management system and its features?
Answer:

Software development and testing teams have several choices of defect management tools to help maintain their defect efforts in software. An overall Defect Management system requires appropriate selection and utilization of an effective tool.

Defect Management systems are a combination of some tools and management process. Ignoring either can result in sub-optimality. The detailed, distinctive standard operating procedures of the defect management process along with policies are carried out. There are a few features to consider while selecting a defect management tool.

There are core features:

   a) To offer a centralized repository for cross projects, defect tracking.

   b) To offer notifications of assignments of resource automatically.

c) The Capability to define defect resolution statuses in order to trace back defect management process.

d) The Capability to provide reports to management, with the number of grouped-open defects such as priority, severity, and project.

There are optional features:
a) Ability to maintain external and internal teams.
b) Ability to capture other items other than defects.
c) Easy to use ability.

186: What is Test Coverage?
Answer:
Test Coverage is a term used to gauge the amount of software programming tests being exercised.
In other words, it is the measurement of the amount of tests performed by a test set usually expressed in percentage. This will normally involve collecting information about parts of a program which are actually executed while running the test suite in order to identify considered conditional statements branches. The formula to calculate the test coverage is:
Test Coverage = [No. of. Items exercised for coverage / Total No. of. Coverage items]*100%
There are many kinds of test coverage:
a) Code
b) Screen item
c) Model
d) Feature
e) Scenario

Each coverage type presumes that some kind of bottom-line exists, which defines the system under test. Therefore, the number of test coverage types varies. The fundamental point of coverage is the code coverage in testing and foremost methodical testing is the path coverage testing. It is important to know that 100% coverage is not equal to 100% testing. Meaning, techniques of coverage measure only single dimension out of a multi dimensional concept.

187: What is a Test Case Design?
Answer:
The work of producing and writing test suites for testing software is known as test design.
A test design needs to have a test case very specifically defined. The detailed and specific input is required. Knowing what the input is supposed to do in the system will enable to tell if the tests have passed or failed. The test case design includes,

   a) Test cases designing with inputs and outputs to test the system.
   b) A set of tests created with the goal to find defects and has effective validation.
   c) Approaches like Partition testing and requirements based testing.

The Test design may require one of the below or all.

   a) Knowledge of the software business and its area of operation.
   b) Functionality knowledge to test.
   c) Testing techniques Knowledge and heuristic knowledge.
   d) Planning skills to schedule the test case order, has to be designed with respect to the effort, cost and time required.

The test suite will have enough test cases for testing the system. The well designed test suites, provides an efficient testing. In this way, there is no time wasted, in writing laid-off test cases that would needlessly consume time whenever they are executed.

188: What is the term 'release', 'build' and 'version' in software testing?
Answer:
Release: The delivery or deployment of the final description of a development application or a product is known as a Release. A

release in the software may either be public or private and usually comprises of the initial production of a new application or an upgraded one. The alpha and beta stages are carried out before a release. Release is the application itself.

Build: In an agile software development method, a release is a software deployable package after the end of several iterations. Releases are also done before the end of the iteration. In the context of programming, a Build is an edition of a completed program. It is a pre release version and is identified by a number, but not by a release number. Re-iterative builds are a chief part of the development process. Throughout the development phase, components of application are collected and frequently compiled for testing purposes and to ensure a final dependable product. Build is a part of the application.

Version – Whenever there is a requirement like changes or addition to the existing requirement of the client, then the number of releases done, according to the requirement is known as a Version. Each Version is given an identification number and name with respect to the previous version. This is the extension of a Build. Version is the application itself.

189: Explain Priority and its types.
Answer:
'Priority' in testing means giving or associating levels for test case results to be handled accordingly with respect to scheduling. 'Priority' is a defect or a test result deviation that deserves or needs former attention. It establishes preferences in order of importance (or pressure) as 'High, Medium and Low'. The word 'priority' comes up in bug tracking system. A range of commercial and problem tracking tools for software management are accessible. A selective tool is used, with the thorough inputs of software tests, which, gives the development team the complete information, so they can understand the bug. With an idea of its 'severity', priority is judged and the bug is reproduced to fix it. Thus, fixing of bugs is based on the project's 'severity' and 'priorities'. The 'severity' of a problem is based on agreement with

the customer's risk assessment and is recorded in their selected tracking tool. Software that has bugs can 'severely' affect schedules and leads to a re-evaluation and negotiation of 'priorities'. Priority is usually of three types.

a) **Low**: The defect is repaired after awaiting more serious defect being fixed.

b) **Medium**: The defect to be resolved in the normal course and can wait until a new version or build is created.

c) **High**: The defect must be resolved at the earliest as it affects the product or the application severely. In this case of defect, the system cannot be used until the repair is done.

Thus, priority is closely associated with severity for resolving bugs and, is solely important to decide test case execution.

190: Explain Severity and its types.
Answer:
'Severity' is a decision making term used to decide for fixing of bugs or defects associated with the standards and customer's need. 'Severity' is the quality or state of being severe, which implies adherence to meticulous standards or elevated principles. This expression often implies harshness. It is the extent to which the bug or defect can influence the software. Otherwise, it defines the impact of a defect in the system. There are a few types of Severity and is also associated with the priority.

a) **Cosmetic**: When the enhancement of the system has changes related to the look and feel of the application, the defect related to that severity is termed as cosmetic.

b) **Minor**: A minor is the term used for defect that does not terminate or damage the usability of the system and the desired results can easily be obtained by a work-around of the defects.

c) **Moderate**: This type of defect might not result in the termination, but the system produces incomplete, inconsistent or incorrect results.

d) **Major**: This type of defect results in the break of one or more component of the system or the whole system. The data can be extensively corrupted and the function fails, which is not usable. But an alternative acceptable method to achieve the required results is possible.

e) **Critical**: This type of defect results in the termination of one or more component of the system or the whole system and data gets extensively corrupted. The failed function has to be immediately fixed as there is no alternative acceptable method and it is not usable to achieve the required results.

191: Give an example of a high severity and low priority.
Answer:
Below is a high severity and low priority example.
Consider a Yahoo login page with 'Username and Password' text boxes and 'Login in' button.
If the 'Login in' button text is not clear to understand or if it is not situated in a proper manner, the user will not know the use of that button. Although the text to read is simple, the placement, manner or the use of the button is not understood. Though the user might be able to proceed further and log into the page, he might not easily do so. This leaves a bad impression of the application on the user in the first instance. Therefore, the bug will have a high severity from the user perspective and have low priority, because the functionality of the button works fine and allows the user to login with a bad impact on the application as a whole. The priority has many types as high, medium and low and this will be determined by the management with respect to other bug severity and priority. In this case of an issue, the management may proceed further to next release without fixing it immediately and decide to fix it at a later stage.

192: Give an example of a high severity and high priority.
Answer:
An error that has both functional and requirement issue of the user or the client will have a high priority and high severity. Here

is an example for High Priority & High Severity.

Consider a 'student details' maintenance website. It has records like academic project, examination result and other activities. Suppose, the student needs to update respective education information like completion of homework, projects and other details. The student clicks on the 'save' button after filling all the details in the record, and the activity performed does not redeem, then the bug is considered as high severity and priority.

This is because, the student invests time to update or change or enter additional details and finds that the effort in doing so is not successful and eventually waste of time. Thus, the students' goals and purpose is not served. This is both a major functionality issue (severity) and business requirement issue (priority). Therefore, it is a high severity and priority that needs to be resolved immediately before the release version. Again, the types of priority and severity are the decision by the management and client based on other defect criteria or production activities.

193: Give an example of a low severity and high priority.
Answer:

Here is an example of low severity and high priority.

Consider a Yahoo login page or the home page which has the yahoo logo on the top of the page. The logo shows up with wrong spelling or missing letters in the spelling. There are three perspectives involved here, from the user point, client point and the production team point of view. The functionality of the page is not affected in any way with the logo. Therefore, it will have a low severity as the impact on the user, is also not high. From the development or software application functionality point of view, the urgency in fixing this type of error may be low. But, the name 'Yahoo' is part of branding for the client, and due to requirement this becomes an issue with high priority. Therefore, it can be called as a low severity bug and high priority defect. The management along with the client decide on the schedule to fix it. Spelling mistakes can happen on the heading or title of an application or on the cover page or anywhere within the product or application. Such obvious mistakes are calculated based on client preference to fix.

194: Give an example of a low severity and low priority.
Answer:
There are a few mistakes that are commonly considered as low severity and priority which do not greatly affect the user or client or the functionality. Below is an example of low severity and low priority.
Consider an existing application or a product that has a small enhancement with respect to updating information and details within the pages along with other functional requirement change. The change with new updated information is added on a certain page or pages. Testing is done prior to the release and defects are logged with respect to cosmetic issues, apart from other functionality issues. The changes with respect to the information on the page within the content (paragraph) of the body (not the title, heading and cover page) are all part of cosmetic enhancement. Suppose there is a spelling error or double letter addition in a word or an unexpected space within a word; then they are considered as small defects. Therefore, the defect becomes low severity and low priority which is not affecting the user activities or any functionality. There is no 'clicking' activity on that page or area and the number of visitors on the page is low. Such fixes can be done at a later stage without major importance.

195: Explain a Test Scenario.
Answer:
The 'requirement' document is the key to frame the Test Scenario. The Test scenario is framed based on the set of test cases or all the conditions which determines the test coverage against the requirement of the business on the whole. Test scenarios cover a number of steps to complete one whole condition (functionality or feature) check. This is different from a Test Case, which has numerous detailed - single steps to check the condition (functionality or feature). Test Scenario ensures checking of end

to end software functionality or business flow of the software. The testers perform testing in the form of end users or real world scenario. Testers can get help from clients or developers or stakeholders to create a Test scenario. Test scenario helps in finding lots of defects with respect to functionality and end user perspective. A test scenario must be identified and then created. A Test scenario is always created first and then each Scenario can be created with test cases.

An example for Test scenario: A Gmail account can have many scenarios like, testing below conditions and more.

a) User authentication on the login page.
b) Email sending operation.
c) Checking Email Inbox.
d) Email Draft folder operation.
e) Spam folder operation.
f) Trash folder operation.
g) 'Chats' folder operation.

196: Explain the Test Scenario and Test case with an example.
Answer:
Below is an example to know the dissimilarity between Test Case and Test Scenario.

Consider an application that has the login screen, with login name, password, and option to remember the password on the page and Login button. Below is the Test Scenario and Test case for the login screen.

Test Scenario: 'User Login activity' – Check for the conditions below and record the respective results.

a) Enter name and Password fields individually.
b) Perform the test with a valid login name and valid password.
c) Perform the test with an invalid login name and valid password.
d) Perform the test with a valid login name and invalid password.
e) Perform the test with an invalid login name and invalid

password.

Many conditions, apart from the above are covered in the Scenario. Considering the 2nd condition from the above, the Test Case can be written in a detailed manner.

Test Case: 'User Login activity'
  a) Open the browser and record results,
  b) Enter the URL in the address bar and enter the actual result,
  c) Check if the login features such as a User name field, Password field, and Login button, is showing up on the loaded page and enter the results,
  d) Enter the all valid Name and password and check for acceptance criteria which should be successful and record the actual results,
  e) Click on the Login button and check the user must successfully enter to Home page upon 'Page Load' and record the result.

197: What are the Test Deliverables?
Answer:

Test deliverables are documents prepared after performing testing of various activities in a software development process such as a test case template, test plan document, and bug report template. The Test Deliverables will be delivered to the client for the completed activities along with the activities, which is implemented for improved productivity with respect to the company's standards.

They are the artifacts, which are also submitted to the stakeholders during the development life cycle. There are diverse test deliverables at every stage of the lifecycle. Test deliverables are offered at different phases like, during the testing phase or before testing phase or after the testing phase. The different Test deliverables may be,
  a) Software Test Plan
  b) Test case Documents

c) Test plan for Automation
d) Test automation scripts
e) Test Coverage and Traceability matrices
f) Defect Matrix
g) Test Results document
h) Test Schedule document (deadlines for deliverables)
i) Test Report or project report (the project delivery to client)
j) Weekly status report (sent by the Project Manager to the client)
k) Release notes or document

198: What is the difference between Testing method and Testing Methodology?
Answer:
There is a difference in Testing Methodology and Testing methods.
Testing Methodology defines a process, principle and a set of rules, which are to be followed by an assigned group of testers by testing the application. Below steps are involved in the Testing Methodology.

a) Requirement Analysis for Testing
b) Test Planning
c) Test Designing
d) Test Execution
e) Tracking Defects
f) Test Automation
g) Test Maintenance

Testing methods can be called as Testing Techniques and there are two main types, White Box Testing and Black Box Testing techniques. Under these two types, Unit Testing, Integration Testing, Functional Testing, System Testing, Performance Testing, Load testing, Volume testing & Security Testing, Stress testing and UAT testing are all performed. Grey box testing, which is a combination of the White box and Black box, can also be considered as a Testing method. These types are ultimate procedures that produce a test result with respect to clarity or quality or measurement.

199: What is a Test Suite?
Answer:
Test suite, is a compilation of test cases that are planned to be used to feed as an input to a software program to ensure that the software has some specified set of behaviors as per the specifications. A test suite habitually contains goals or thorough instructions for every collection of test case. It also holds information to be used on the system configuration, for testing. A collection of test cases may also contain steps or prerequisite states and descriptions. Collections of test cases may also be called as a test scenario or even a test script. A test suite is executable when it is ready or completed. This means that usually a test exploit exists that is integrated with the suite, such that the test harness and the test suite jointly can work on an adequately detailed level, to communicate correctly with the system under test. A test suite can also be used for some specific functionality in the system. The test suite is useful for carrying out Build verification tests, Functional test, Regression test, and smoke and Integration tests.

200: What is a test report and content of test report?
Answer:
Test Report is a document that is prepared at a certain phase. A Test report is generally prepared once the product is rolled out to the client. This document is usually prepared by the Team Lead or a Project manager and delivered to the client. Primarily, this document describes the process undertaken in the project, accomplished achievements, outcomes of the project and knowledge acquired and more. The Test report is also known as the 'Project Closure Report'. All the activities that took place throughout the project are summarized. The contents enclosed in the Test Report are,

    a) **Test Environment** – The details such as the web servers or Application, OS, Database, Machine names and more that is used for the project are mentioned.

b) **Testing Methods** – Types of Tests like Functional Testing, Platform Testing, and regression testing, and more are mentioned.

c) **Bug Tracking** – The inflow and outflow details of the 'bus' in the delivered project is mentioned.

d) **Work schedule** – The start and end time of the testing is mentioned.

e) **The Defect Analysis report should contain**
    i) Defects reported under Functional Test and Regression Test.
    ii) The Defects' state at the end of the Test cycle.
    iii) RCA - Root cause analysis for the bug tag as 'not a bug'.

f) **Quality Assurance observations made throughout the life cycle.**

201: What is a high level and low level test case?
Answer:
The high level Test Case covers the main functionalities like to create, edit, delete and more.

The low level Test Case covers the web or an application screen, with respect to input fields to display as per the requirements such as, button's appearance (enabled / disabled), and low priority functionalities.

Below are a few 'high level Test Case' and 'low level test cases'. Consider a screen with two edit boxes as login and password; Push buttons as 'OK and Reset'; 'Check box' with the label to read as 'Store my password'.

High Level Test Case:
a) Check that the User is able to login with a valid login and a valid password.

b) Check that the User is not able to login with an invalid login and a valid password and vice-versa.

c) Check that the User is not able to login with an invalid login and invalid password.

   d) Check that the pop up message is shown, for a blank login.
   e) Check that the Reset button functionality clears the filled screen.

Low Level Test Case:
   a) Verify the launched URL of the application displays the below attributes on the screen.
       i)   'Login Name' field
       ii) Password' field
       iii) 'OK' button
       iv) 'RESET' button
       v)   The label as 'Store my password' with check box provided should be unchecked.
   b) Check that the OK button is 'disabled' until the login name and password fields are entered.
   c) Check that the OK button is 'enabled' once the login name and password fields are entered.
   d) Check that the User is able to tick mark the 'check box' under the label 'Store my pwd'

In this way, many more test cases can be written and can be classified between 'high level' and 'low level'.

202: What is the database testing?
Answer:
The Database (D testing validates for the below attributes.
   a) Validation of the field size.
   b) Indexing for performance related issues are done or not.
   c) Check constraints.
   d) Stored procedures.
   e) The defined field size in the application should match with that in the DB.
   f) All the data from the application has to be properly inserted into the database. Otherwise, it imposes constraints on the data, like, database integrity.
   g) Should check for various data with respect to DB performance, functionality and loading. DB testing should also check and remove the data redundancy.

h)   Under manual DB testing, the query is typed to see if the table is providing the same result or not.

i)   Check for retrieving of the data, by giving some selected statements and simultaneously insert data, through 'insert statements' in the database. Check the effects.

Database testing is done in two ways, one via front-end and the other through backend end. Inserting the values in the front-end of the application and checking the data is stored in the database. And inserting the data in the database (backend) and checking if the data is displayed in the application.

203: How to write and document a Test case?
Answer:
The Test case, documents the functional requirements. The planned audience of the Test case document is the project team, project manager, and the testing team. Some portions of the test case document may occasionally be shared with the client or user and other stakeholders, whose approval or inputs into the testing process are needed. The test case documentation includes the below.

a)   **Test Case Specification** - The test case to be performed is described.

b)   **Description** - The test case and the testing individuals involved in the testing, is described. It also includes diagrams demonstrating the interaction between individuals and the different elements being tested.

c)   **Post Conditions** - The post conditions are described in the use case. A post state or condition means a list of possible situations that is present in the system, soon after the test case has been finished.

d)   **Preconditions** - The test case preconditions are described. The state of the system must be live before a test case can be executed and this is known as a precondition.

e)   **Resources** - The testers involved in the testing, their association and responsibilities, with the test case are described.

f) **Exclusion or Inclusion of test inputs** - Test cases that need to be included or excluded in the execution of the test case is listed.

g) **Events** - The flow of events expected in the normal conditions and any alternative potential flow of events, and errors or exceptions that may be expected are listed.

h) **Unique Requirements** - Special requirements that may be necessary to perform the test case is listed.

204: What are the different Testing environments?
Answer:

There are a few types of testing environments. They are:

a) **The development environment** – Is the programming environment. The developers use this environment for building the software.

b) **QA Environment** – This environment is used by the Testing team to test the developed build without affecting development work. There is a slight difference from the development environment, to ensure the development work is not disturbed. Thus, allowing the two teams to perform their work efficiently.

c) **Production Environment** – The software has finally reached the desired person, which is the User. The machine which is used by the User has the final product or software running. This is known as Production Environment. Testing is done to ensure that the necessary tools are installed in the user end, as installed on the developer's machines. This ensures proper setup and installation which is the actual environment used by the organization.

d) **Live environment** – The software or product is ready to be used by the end users on the internet. This is similar to the production environment, but with slightly wider audience like the web.

e) **Staging Environment** – In some situations, the staging environment is same as the Testing environment. This also constitutes for a similarity of the production environment where an upgrade or a lot of changes or enhancement are going into the production. The adjustments like changing of staging into production mode can be easily made to handle a given situation.

f) **Test Environment** – This environment consists of hardware, software and security. This setup close to production or the live environment to tap on any unnoticed behavior.

Some of the above environments might be similar with the purpose of use. These terminologies are used based on the process nature and situation in a project.

205: What are the types of Design Documentation?
Answer:
There are two types of Design documentation.

Low Level Design Documentation (LLD): This level deals with basic or lower level modules. The data flow diagram is handled here by the developers. The team divides the total application into modules in this designing. There is at least one document for each module. The logic is derived for each module and hence LLD is also known as detailed design. The internals of the individual modules is designed in pseudo code which is identified during High level designing. Programming specs are enclosed under LLD. Every specific module is described in a detailed manner, and enables the program to be directly coded by the developer. The algorithms and data structure of the modules are documented. Class diagrams are drawn in relation between classes and all the methods. This design also contains database tables with all elements with the size and type, all interface details with API references with responses and requests, listings of error message, all dependent issues; entire input and output of a module.

High Level Design Documentation (HLD): HLD is a design with respect to higher level modules. It has a flow diagram with an Entity Relationship. The Testers and Developers are both involved to handle this Level. The team organizes functional architecture known as a functional flow for designing this. High level design involves a decaying system into modules, and representing the invocation and interfaces relationships among modules. This design is referred to as software architecture. A HLD document will usually include a high level architecture diagram representing the components, networks, and interfaces that are further developed. The document may also refer to work flows or data flows between component systems.

206: Write test cases for functional testing for the website page 'Google.com'.
Answer:
Consider the Google page (web page with applications) with the URL as 'google.com'. Below is the functional test case template and details that will be written and included.

Release version: V10.8.2.0

Tester Name: XYZ

Total number of Test cases: 8

Test Case: Google Search Home page

Note: NA – Not applicable

SN	Test Scenario	Description	Input Value	Expected result	Actual result	Status: Pass/Fail
	Google Search page: Check for necessary labels, buttons, Logo, links as per the requirement.	Enter 'Google.com' in the address bar and click Enter button on the keyboard.	Google.com	Check the loaded Google search page for a. 'Google Country Icon' in the middle of the page, b. A text box to enter inputs, c. Search by voice icon, d. Google search button, e. I'm feeling lucky -button. f. '+You, Gmail, Images, Apps Icon' should show on the right top corner of the page. g. Links at the bottom of the page for different language options.	(To be executed)	(To be executed)
1		Place the mouse over the '+You' link. Click on '+you' link.	NA	Upon the user click action, the page should load and show 'Google – Choose an account' page.		
2		Mouse over on 'Gmail' Clickable link should show on the right top corner on the page. Place the mouse on the 'Gmail' link.	NA	Clicking on 'Gmail' link should show the loaded page of the user's 'Gmail logged into an email account' page.		
3		'Images' Clickable link should show on the right top corner of the page. Place the mouse on the 'Images' link.	NA	Upon Clicking the link, should show the loaded page 'Goggle search with an images' page.		
4		The apps clickable ' Icon' should be shown on top right corner of the window page. Place the mouse on the 'Icon' link.	NA	Upon clicking the Icon, the Apps text label should show a window with Google's 9 Icons for other applications'.		
5		'Sign in' blue button on the right top corner of the page should be shown and be clickable. Place the mouse on the 'Sign in' button.	NA	Clicking on the button should load a refreshed page as 'Choose an account or Sign in'.		
6.		Enter user inputs like alphabets or numeric or characters in the text box.	Say, "Gmail account login"	Click on 'Google search' button. The refreshed page should show a number of links with many page results with a topmost link as 'mail.google.com'.		
7.		Click on 'I'm feeling lucky' button	NA	Should show a refreshed page with Doodles themes.		
8.		Click on each language option next to label 'Google.co.in offered in...'	NA	Each language should show a refreshed Google search page with respective languages.		

The above is the way to write a test case and 'Actual result and Status' will be available and entered after the execution of the Test case.

Testing Industries

207: What is Automation in testing and how did it evolve?
Answer:
Software testing tasks, such as extensive regression testing become arduous and consume time to perform manual testing. Therefore, a manual testing approach might not always be the answer in finding certain defect classes. Automation testing offers an opportunity to perform repeated functionality testing and non-functional testing effectively. After the development of automated tests, they can be run repeatedly and quickly to save time. Mostly this can be a cost effective means for regression testing with an extended maintenance life of a software product. Minor areas of the application which worked well at an earlier point in time, can cause features to shatter over the lifetime. Test automation has two general approaches.

a) GUI - Graphical user interface testing.
b) The Code has driven testing.

Automation testing is available in the industry in the various forms of tools and can be expensive. They are both available as a Freeware or Licensed with different frameworks. They are usually engaged functioning in a combination with manual testing. 'Automation testing' in the long term can be made cost effective, particularly when repeatedly used in regression testing.

208: What are the major Automated Industry Standard Testing Frameworks?
Answer:
Below are the industry standard designs for testing automation, which is considered as frameworks.

a) Query Driven Automation
b) Keyword Driven Automation
c) Data Driven Automation
d) Model Driven Automation

Sometimes, there are more than one of the above designs is used for the automation testing approach. Other approaches used are

Hybrid and Modular Automation. Hybrid automation is used for multiple projects and extended time limits formed of a number of function libraries or reusable modules. 'Modular Automation' is also referred to as Component Based Design for Test Case. There is a product known as 'Business Process Testing' and it consists of,

a) Business Components that are reusable

b) Business Components that are converted into test process

In this framework, components are reusable units, which performs a detailed job in a business process such as 'Add to Cart' feature and more. A 'business process testing' consists of test scenarios with business components such as 'Place an Order' and so on. These are a few industry standards' automated testing frameworks.

209: Why testing is needed in the financial industry?
Answer:
The financial services industry is under attack from numerous and significant Cyber criminal threats. The violation data (in numbers) reveal that records containing 'personally identifiable information (PII)' are being stolen each year. Banks are assigning resources with additional care due to the present, ever competitive pressure and economic strain to operate efficiently. This may lack the unity and alleviate existing deficiencies in process controls and basic operation.

In place of allocating resources, penetration testing is substituted as detective control that can emphasize areas of risk overloaded by system administrators accidentally creating vulnerabilities. The scope of Penetration testing must be clearly and carefully articulated. The scope may need to be pointed to include a subset of business units or specific technology targets before beginning any work. For instance, a unit of business that has business partner's network connections will be given first priority. The scope included here is a test of all wired and wireless networks, and Web applications, in that business line. This includes three options: out source, in source and a hybrid testing approach, through which a financial institution may build up some in house skills and outsource skills that require specialization.

210: What is outsourced testing in the industry?
Answer:
Outsourcing in Software Testing is carried out by an independent team or a company who is not involved directly in the course of software development. Software testing is a necessary phase of software development; and often viewed as a non core activity by most organizations. Outsourcing allows a company to focus on its core development activities, while the independent validation work is handled by the exterior software testing experts. Many business benefits like, an independent assessment (leads to superior delivery confidence); lower investment infrastructure, time reduced to market, predictable quality software, not risking low deadlines and increased time for development is offered. There are different Software Testing Outsourcing forms available.

a) Availability of additional resources for major projects
b) Utilizing determined specialist groups for Beta stage User Acceptance Testing coordinated by an outdoor organization
c) Complete outsourcing of the test process from planning, strategy, execution and conclusion. This is referred to as a 'Managed Testing Service'
d) Tests are often related to stress, load or performance testing.

Thus, a trained- independent team of software testing engineers outsourced, may provide the utmost benefit but with a slightly higher cost.

211: What is on-site and offshore testing?
Answer:
Testing software is time consuming and labour exhaustive activity and is extremely necessary for the Company's achievement. On-site or offshore model is a very common working process for various IT teams across the industry, particularly the QA teams.

An on-site means working at the client geographical location. One or limited QA team service provider's member, will work alongside with the customer (client) at their location depending on the extent of the project. This member is commonly known as the On-site QA coordinator. The service company's work place and the client location can be across the globe, geographically in any place. Typically, Offshore means working from the location other than the client such as another office space within the same geographical area or office outside the geographical area. The decision is made by the company (project owner) based on cost, time consuming or skills or efficiency to perform the testing. There are some viewpoints from the Offshore and On-site resources respectively.

a) This model can ensure that there is continuing work for every minute on a project if used correctly.
b) Direct client interaction helps easy availability of requirements and the system information. It also helps in healthier communication, thus improving the business relationship.
c) It is cost effective to have offshore teams with less cost, than setting up the entire on-site QA team.

212: What are the On-site and Offshore testing responsibilities?
Answer:
Below are the responsibilities of an On-site QA coordinator:
a) Vice versa communication is carried out for progress, time lines, delays and more, between the client and the team.
b) Technical knowledge is obtained and transferred from the client to the production or test team
c) Shares the 'functional requirements' document and makes a test plan
d) Inputs are provided on the test data preparation phase
e) A sign off is provided after reviewing the Test cases or Test scenarios with the client team.
f) Test execution guidelines are provided and occasionally found participating in the test execution

g) The sanity and smoke test is performed on the deployed build and sign off is provided to continue testing for the test team

h) Defect review meetings are held with the concerned support and development teams

i) UAT (user acceptance testing) Support is provided

j) Metrics are collected

Below are the responsibilities of the Offshore team:

a) The associates work on test scenarios after getting the test plan

b) After sign off of the test scenarios, the team works on the test case documentation

c) Test data is prepared

d) Tests are executed

e) Defects are reported

f) Test reports are prepared

g) Inputs are provided for collection of test metric

h) Defect review and project related meetings' participation

213: What is e-commerce testing?

Answer:

E-commerce application which is a web application, by nature provides synchronized access to shared resources. That is, the servers on which e-commerce is hosted should be able to respond to multiple users over the same period of time requesting for the same resources. As a fact, during development, the application appears to behave right for 'click through' web pages in the browser. The typical e-commerce product page template includes a lot of information like, details and specifications, a description, photos of the product, and often options for the customer to choose from, such as colour and different models or sizes. Therefore, understanding the most important feature in the decision making process of a visitor is the key for success. This is often different for one website versus others.

The conversion plan for optimization should address the entire customer prospective in all of their flights through the website such as,

a) Detail Pages of the 'Product'
b) Page for 'Category'
c) Page for 'Home'
d) Constant Action Calls
e) Forms

Apart from functional test, browser testing is a key aspect of e-commerce website. With the range of testing tools available such as JMeter, A/B tests and more can be used for testing an e-commerce site.

214: What are the features for testing e-commerce site?
Answer:
Below are some common features to test the e-commerce site. Testing is done to check everything that negatively affects the site.

a) Within the CSS style sheet changes are formatted.
b) Beyond simple descriptive text with content changes - promotional banners, images in sliders, and headlines.
c) Changing Settings that may impact the checkout, such as collected data, payments, and cart, links, and check out promotions.
d) Adding content to the secure checkout screens.
e) To make sure promotion is not expired nor has out of stock items.
f) Testing regularly for adding or removing links (for cross links checking that may break when a promotion expires or an item is removed).
g) Changes to Site navigation.
h) Modifications of Template.
i) Added or modified Forms.
j) Shipping Settings changes made.
k) Adding Promotional Coupons.
l) Discounts on Volume.
m) Changes to Login process.
n) Added or removed landing pages.
o) Specific landing pages that are pointed to 'new ad

campaigns'.

p) Up-gradation or change to System or application software.

q) Changes related to major browser or operating system which affects the clients, such as implementation of IE 10, Windows updates, major releases of Safari, Chrome, and Firefox.

Standards of Testing

215: What are the standards of software testing?
Answer:
Quality is always observed from two sides, from a producer viewpoint and a consumer viewpoint.

As a consumer, everyday lives depend on safe and quality products and good standards are considered as healthy. The standard represents a guarantee to the customer/consumer that the product is of a good quality. There is also a reasonable expectation of safety and cost with a balance between the two of the product/service. Thereby, a producer is more likely to avoid the pitfalls of legal liability and bad publicity for selling 'insecure' products. Sometimes due to standards, a new manufacturer need not have to start from scratch, but can build on the standard's experience written by the authors. There are very wide varying quality standard's authors and it is difficult to find out the worth reading. There are standards relevant to software testing, but some important areas, such as integration testing has no useful standard existing at all. However, any knowledgeable standards' use, will improve the software tester's effectiveness.

There are two ways to identify software testing standards.

 a) As part of a larger requirement, standards are considered as a mandate for testing. These are for those who want to state useful agreement with a standard, such as ISO 9000.

 b) Software testing is also supported in parts by Standards and is covered. These are of more use to actual performing testers, who do not want to start from the scratch each time a new area of responsibility is given.

Thus, there are a lot of standards to use for and choosing is done appropriately.

216: Explain about an Audit.
Answer:
The definition of an 'Audit' generally means a documented and well planned activity executed by qualified personnel such as the Auditor, for various activities. This involves determining by examination, evaluation, or investigation of objective evidence,

the compliance and adequacy with applicable documents, or established procedures, and the efficiency of implementation. The term 'Audit' may refer to assessment in internal controls, accounting, project management, quality management, energy conservation, and water management.

In other words, Auditing is an independent and systematic examination of statements, data, operations, performances and records of a project for a stated purpose. The Auditor, in any Auditing, perceives and identifies the propositions for examination before hand, collects evidence and evaluates the same. With this as a base, the judgment is formulated which is then communicated via Audit report. The intention is to give an opinion on the sufficiency of the controls within an environment of Audition, to assess and improve the efficacy of risk control, governance processes, and risk management. Auditing is done in two ways, external audit and internal audit.

217: What is Process Audit?
Answer:
The Process Audit is to ensure that the process of the product is made of the defined plan or procedure or arrangement. The Process Audit involves the checklist items to be achieved as below.

   a)   Purchase of raw materials from an approved supplier
   b)   Materials should be inspected as per the requirements
   c)   Standardized gages must be used
   d)   Materials in the storage must be correctly labelled and protected
   e)   Proper instructions must be followed for inventory such as rotation, handling, and more
   f)   As per the control plan, the part should be made on the correct machine
   g)   SPC – Statistical Process Control, should be done as per the defined control plan
   h)   Process rate should be as per the requirements
   i)   Quality levels must meet requirements

j)   All steps should be followed in the proper order of the 'Control plan'
k)   Inspection of requirements must be followed
l)   The Nonconforming product must follow procedure as necessary

218: What is Product Audit?
Answer:

The Product Audit means measures to ensure product meets all the specifications.

The Product Audit is the assessment of the final product or service and its qualification for use evaluated against the product or service intention. By meticulously inspecting the final product, it aims at increasing profitability, improving quality, and enhancing loyalty and satisfaction, before delivering to a customer or a supplier. In order to establish the product meets specifications, it is necessary for it to go through this process. Ultimately, the Product Audit serves as an advantage to the customers and suppliers, by ensuring quality and resulting in higher customer satisfaction.

The Audit involves a few checklist items to be achieved.

a)   All dimensions or specifications should be correct.
b)   The product should be checked for any damage, before packing and delivery.
c)   The product must have a proper container or box.
d)   The container should have proper label.
e)   All the paperwork must be completed properly.

219: What are the advantages of Product Audit in an industry?
Answer:

Other industry benefits of Product Audit are:

a)   Companies and businesses get determined with the product Audit assistance, if the organization is doing what it promises to be.
b)   Through this Audit, organizations and business management can take corrective action for improvement.

c) Quality is established to the extent of the business concerns and a vital quality system is created, if products have to have high quality.

d) It helps in conducting own internal Audits for businesses and companies even before external auditors are involved.

e) Due to some consistent issues with the product, the Audit helps increase customer satisfaction, especially when requested for the same by the customers.

f) The Audit helps in drafting a quality policy for higher business and organization managements.

g) It determines samples by performing random sampling for an accurate demonstration of a company's quality system.

h) This helps in documentation and description of tasks and specific activities of an organization, to ensure great quality products.

i) The extent of quality concerned product is determined and distinguished with the difference between non conformance and observation.

j) It strives to meet difficult objectives by constantly measuring the effectiveness of current processes and satisfies customers.

k) It helps to gather information that relates to the product and process qualities and its system.

l) Creates a 'forum' of audit team consisting of the Auditor and Auditee to be able to discuss the results of a product.

m) When the Audit is conducted by an external Auditor, an objective assessment of quality system's effectiveness is obtained.

n) As per the requirement of ISO 9000, Product Audit helps conducting internal Audits of products by the organization's own staff.

o) Helps address adequate quality issues to sell products competitively with an edge over other products.

220: What is SPC?

Answer:

SPC can be expanded as the 'Statistical process control'. SPC is one of the quality control methods which use statistical methods. SPC is useful in order to control and monitor a process. This process ensures that SPC operates at its complete potential. At this point, the process can make the most of product conforming, to the least of waste like scrap or rework. The SPC method can be applied for a process to the conforming product (specifications met by the product) output being measured. In SPC, the major tools used include the focus on constant improvement; control charts; and the experiment's design. The practices of SPC are in two phases - The initial phase is the establishment of the process, and the secondary phase is the regular process production. During the second phase, the period of examination is decided, based on the changes in the conditions such as Man, Material, Machine, and Method. Also decision is made based on 'wear and tear' rate of product parts used in manufacture like, Jigs, machine parts, and tools standards and fixture. A common process where SPC is applied is in the product manufacturing department.

221: What is the basic ISO testing standard?

Answer:

ISO can be expanded as 'International Organization for Standards'. There are ISO 9001, 9002, and 9003 standards and are anxious quality systems that are gauged by Outside Auditors. Apart from just software, they are also applied to many kinds of manufacturing and production organizations. The most widespread standard is ISO 9001, and is most often used by software development institutes. It covers design, documentation, production, development, installation, testing, servicing, and other processes. ISO 9000-3 (different from 9003), is an education for applying ISO 9001 series to software development organizations. The standard of the U.S. version of the ISO 9000 series is called as the ASQ Q9000 / ANSI series. This U.S. version series can be purchased directly from the 'American Society for

Quality (ASQ)' or the ANSI organizations. To obtain an ISO 9001 certification, which is normally good for about 3 years, is done by a third party Auditor assessing an organization. After 3 years, a complete reassessment is necessary. Importantly, an ISO 9000 certification does not essentially indicate quality of products, but it only indicates that processes are followed as per documentation.

222: Explain Quality System.
Answer:
The direction for the corporate are provided by the quality system and are interwoven with most departments of a business. Such systems enable a company to effectively scrutinize customer complaints, inspect the root cause of issues and authorize manufacturing processes.

A quality system is a collection of the organizational activities, processes and procedures, plans, incentives, policies, resources and responsibilities, and the infrastructure necessary in formulating and employing a total quality management approach. These systems are a fundamental component in industries, anxious with regard to customer satisfaction and safety. A quality system consists of various divisions that are responsible for certifying that the objectives of the entire system are met. This is achieved by the executing strong-broad standard operating procedures and an internal audit scheduled program. These actions are performed by every employee, thereby decreasing the occurrence of an error. The 'corporate' is also responsible for identifying the 'root cause analysis (RCA)' for problems and providing solutions for the same to prevent them from happening again. The Quality system can also be known as Quality management system. A few QMS regime methods used in the industries are simple statistics, random sampling, ISO 9000, ISO 19011 and more.

223: Explain Total Quality Management.
Answer:
TQM is expanded as 'Total Quality Management'. TQM is a

widespread and ordered approach that seeks improvement of the quality of products/services through ongoing enhancements in reaction to the organizational management continuous feedback. TQM requirements may be defined individually for an organization or in observance to established standards such as, ISO 9000 (the International Organization for Standardization's) series. TQM can be useful to any type of organization; it is personalized in almost every type of organization to use, including highway maintenance, schools, churches, hotel management and more. According to present e-business, TQM is focused from the customer's point of view on quality management.

The processes for TQM are separated into four sequential categories - planning, doing, checking, and acting. This is known as the PDCA (plan-do-check-act). In the first phase, members define the troubles to be addressed, collect appropriate data, and ascertain the issues' root cause. In the second phase, a solution is developed and implemented by the members, and finalize on a measurement to gauge its efficiency. In the third phase, members confirm the results through pre-and-post data comparison. In the fourth phase, members document their results, process changes are informed to others, and recommend the difficulty to be tackled in the next PDCA cycle.

Therefore, TQM aims at long term success through customer satisfaction, society and also its members.

224: Explain Quality Policy.
Answer:
A company's top management issues a statement known as 'Quality Policy' which states 'the objectives' of the company with regard to manufacture or supply of a service/product that meet the expectations of the customer. Therefore, the quality policy is the commitment of the company (or top management) towards the customer to ensure agreement with the 'quality management system'. Thus, this increases continuous customer satisfaction in making a business relationship with the company. This should be

an underlying understanding of a company's employees with their management and quality expert's decision and be aware of the objectives stated in the quality policy with respect to their responsibilities. Quality policy is similar to QMS, which forces implementation, monitor's efficiency, guides work, allows perceptions, and assumes future. The overall quality policy towards QMS is the management's commitment. Quality policy management is a long term strategic issue and regularly has a ten year scope. There are many methods and ISO 9001 is one of quality policy methods.

225: Explain Quality Circle.
Answer:
A quality circle is a group of composed workers, who volunteer (such as students or others) and operate under the leadership of their superior (team leader). They are educated to recognize, analyze and resolve work relevant trouble. They present their solutions for trouble in the management of the organization to improve their performance, and motivate and improve the work of employees. Once the organization reaches the maturity level, quality circles from within, become self managing after gaining the management confidence. Quality circles are a substitute to the firm concept of labour division, where workers operate in a compartmentalized role and more narrow scope.
Quality circles are classically more formal groups. They regularly meet on company time and are trained by competent persons (generally chosen as facilitators). They may be industrial relations specialists and personnel trained in the basic skills of problem identification and human factors, gathering information and its analysis, basic statistics, and solution generation.

226: Explain Quality Audit in Software Industry.
Answer:
The method of the methodical assessment of a quality system, executed by an external or internal Auditor or sometimes by the team of audits is known as the 'Quality Audit'. It is a vital part of

the organization's quality system, and is a means in the ISO standards for quality system (say, ISO 9001).

Audits in an organization are normally performed on a set of defined periods and would want to certify that there is an obviously defined-internal monitoring measure of the system, which is connected to effective action. This can conclude if the association abides by the defined system quality processes and engage results or procedural based estimation criteria.

After the up gradation of the series of the ISO 9000 standards, the Audit's focus from merely procedural adherence has transferred towards the real value of measurement of the Quality Management System (QMS). Later, through the QMS implementation, the results are gained.

Quality Audits uses variety of software or self assessment tools for an essential management,
   a) Used for objective proof verification of procedures,
   b) To gauge the successfulness of implementing processes,
   c) For judging and achieving any definite target level effectiveness,
   d) To offer suppression in the areas of problem and evidence for reduction.

Quality auditing not only reports for corrective actions and non-fulfillment of requirements, but it points in areas for fine practice requirements. Accordingly, departments distribute information and alter their working tradition by contributing improvement constantly.

227: What is an IEEE testing standard?
Answer:
IEEE can be expanded as 'Institute of Electrical and Electronics Engineers'. The IEEE describes itself as the world's largest society of technical professionals,
   a) Promoting the development and appliance of technology in electrical and electronic sectors,
   b) In allied sciences for the human benefits,
   c) The advancement of the profession, and

d) The well being of the members.

The IEEE fosters the standards of development, such that it develops into international and national standards. A number of journals are published by the organization in local chapters, in special areas such as the IEEE Computer Society and in several large societies. The IEEE standards are created.

IEEE/ANSI 829-1983 - IEEE for Test Documentation Software Standard.

IEEE/ANSI 1008-1987 - IEEE for Unit Testing Software Standards.

IEEE/ANSI 730 - IEEE for Software Quality Assurance Standard Plans.

IEEE / ANSI 1012-1986 - IEEE for Software Verification & Validation Standard Plans.

IEEE / ANSI 1059-1993 - IEEE Guide for Software Validation & Verification Plans and more.

228: Mention different IEEE testing standards.
Answer:
The different standards related to testing processes and QA are mentioned.

IEEE 829 – This is a standard for the documents, formatting used in different phases of software testing.

IEEE 1061 – This defines a methodology for identifying, quality requirements, establishment, analyzing, implementing, and validating the product and process of software quality metrics.

IEEE 1059 – This is a guide for Software Validation and Verification Plans.

IEEE 1008 – This is a unit testing standard.

IEEE 1012 – This is a Software Verification and Validation standard.

IEEE 1044-1 – This is a guide to the software anomaly classification.

IEEE 1028 – This is a software inspection standard.

IEEE 1044 – This is software anomalies classification standard.

IEEE 830 – This is a specifications guide for developing system requirements.

IEEE 730 – This is a standard plan for software quality assurance.

IEEE 1061 – This is a software quality metrics and methodology standard.

IEEE 12207 – This outlines a software life cycle data and life cycle processes standards.

BS 7925-1 – This defines the vocabulary of software testing terms used.

BS 7925-2 – This defines a software component testing standard.

229: What is ANSI, CMMI and SEI testing standards?
Answer:

ANSI can be expanded as 'American National Standards Institute', the primary body of industry standards in the U.S., issues some standards related in software, combined with the IEEE and The American Society for Quality (ASQ). ANSI assists the development of 'American National Standards' and is called as ANS by accrediting the procedures of developing organization's standards. The accreditation of ANSI signifies that the measures used by standards setting organizations meet the Institute's requirements. U.S. standards are coordinated with international standards by the organization so that the American products are used worldwide.

CMMI is Capability maturity model integration and is a methodology or an approach for refining and improving the software development process in an organization. It is a collection of structured practices or a process model. It guides for the process improvement across a division, project or an entire organizational structure. It allows companies to integrate functions that are conventionally separate, set process goals and priorities, provide guidance for quality processes and be the point of reference for process appraising. The CMMI was first developed at the 'Software engineering Institute (SEI)'. Later on CMMI versions were released with three integration levels for development, services and acquisition.

SEI is 'Software Engineering Institute', initiated by the U.S.

Defense Department again to help improve development processes of the software. It aimed to judge the maturity level of the organization in this process. The certification program is built on the basis of performance standards, developed by most noteworthy organizations.

230: What are the levels of CMM/CMMI standard?
Answer:
CMM has 5 levels of model of organizational 'maturity' that determine in delivering quality software effectively. It caters to large organizations such as Defense Department contractors of U.S and more. Anyhow, many of the QA processes involved are suitable for any organization, and can be helpful if reasonably applied. CMM ratings are received by undergoing qualified Auditor's assessments by organizations.

Level 1 – This level is characterized by periodic panics, chaos, and therefore brave efforts are required by individuals to complete projects successfully. Few processes, if any, in place may not be repeatable with successes.

Level 2 – This level needs, requirements management, reasonable planning, tracking software project, and management processes in configuration are all in place. Here, practices can be repeated if successful.

Level 3 – At this level, maintenance processes and software development standard are integrated throughout an organization. A Group of Software Engineering Process is in place, to supervise training programs, and software processes are used to guarantee compliance and understanding.

Level 4 – This level has metrics used, to track products, processes, and productivity. Performance of project is predictable while quality is constantly high.

Level 5 –The last level has the focus on continuous improvement of process. The impact of new technologies and processes can be predicted and successfully implemented as required.

This page is intentionally left blank

Devices Testing

231: What are types of mobile application testing?

Answer:

There are types of testing in Mobile application.

a) **Laboratory Testing** - Usually, the complete wireless network is simulated and testing should be done by network carriers. This testing finds out faults when a mobile application performs some functions by using data or voice connection.

b) **Functional Testing** - Testing should ensure that the working of the application is as per the requirements based on the call flows and user interface.

c) **Performance Testing** - It is testing the application performance under certain conditions such as low memory (space), low battery, no network coverage, plenty of users simultaneously accessing the application server and other conditions are tested. Performance can be affected from two sides and is tested on both client side and application server side.

d) **Memory Leakage Testing** – Testing is vital for the correct functioning of an application, as mobile devices face restriction of memory availability. Due to which a software program or application is unable to manage memory it is allocated in and results in poor performance (of the application) and slows down the overall system.

e) **Usability testing** – Usability Testing is executed to verify if the application is attaining its objectives and getting a positive response from users. This testing is important to determine the application's commercial success (like being user friendly).

f) **Installation testing** – Testing verifies that the installation process is smooth without the user complexities. This testing includes installation, updates and un-installation of an application.

g) **Certification Testing** - Every mobile device is tested against the procedure set by different mobile platforms to get certified (through CMAT exam) for compliance.

h) **Interrupt Testing** - Several interruptions are faced with an application like, out of network coverage and recovery and incoming calls. Below are different types of interruptions.

   i)   Receiving and Outgoing – Calls, MMS, and SMS

   ii) Notifications Incoming

   iii) Removal of Battery

   iv) Data transfer through cable – removal and insertion of cable

   v) Network coverage - outage and recovery

   vi) On/Off of Media Player

   vii) Power cycle of Device

232: Why is Mobile application testing done?
Answer:

Mobile application testing is crucial. It is important to ensure that the customers have an optimistic experience when they use a mobile brand and its applications. The user experience with the application has to be great for every consumer at every time right from the beginning. This is to ensure that the customer's investment should not be wasted and that a customer's bad review can severely affect the business. On the other hand, unlike a testing team, customers are not equipped with testing knowledge and do not have the tools or the time to report back with issues.

The goal of testing is to understand the quality and end user requirements being offered. Testing the mobile application has unique challenges. These challenges provide with skills that is required for making choices about the merge of different techniques and modes to use in testing. Each testing, selection will have advantages and disadvantages associated with it, probably to find that multiple testing choices are required for a complete satisfaction. Therefore, a testing strategy that combines different testing options might be considered, that together provide the best overall result and balances the quality, cost, and marketing time.

233: How do mobile technologies affect testing?
Answer:
Mobile is a booming device with thousands of mobile models and numerous operating systems in the market. Thus, applications may have disadvantages and will not work right every time. Therefore, testing a mobile application is a major challenge. One of the major factors is the mobile usability features and different brands available in the market. This kind of domain testing is greater than web application and desktop testing. The difficulty involved in testing a mobile, is examined in detail.

a) There is a smaller screen on a mobile as compared to a computer or PC

b) There is a smaller footprint on the mobile as compared to a computer

c) Deploying OS on other devices such as Windows, BB, iOS, Android, and more have compatibility issues

d) The OS has versions such as 5.x, BB4.x, iOS5.x, and so on

e) Devices have Keypads such as virtual keypad and hard keypad

f) There are many manufactured mobile devices such as Micromax, Sony Ericsson, LG, Samsung, and Nokia, and so on.

g) It is tough to guarantee if an application works well on a particular device or other device, even though it belongs to the same product brand (makers) family. This is due to the difference in memory allocation, networking factors, screen resolutions, OS optimization, CPU and hardware.

All these factors affect testing and thus testing a mobile is not only difficult but cannot give a complete affirmation.

234: Explain the features for testing mobile application.
Answer:
Due to the variety of 'mobile' features and devices and various mobile platforms, testing mobile applications significantly differs from the standard approach.
Below are the features that must be considered while testing

mobile application for the devices.

a) The strength of consumption of power with respect to the charger charging) sensitivity
b) Memory Operations and memory leakage control
c) Disk space utility for stability in the limited space on the drive
d) Disk space utility for logging activity and working on memory cards
e) Using an optimal Internet connection for - USB, Active Sync, Wi-Fi GPRS, working under unstable connection conditions.
f) To provide support for portrait, landscape modes and various screen resolutions
g) The application stability for - sending and receiving MMS or SMS and incoming or outgoing calls
h) Compliance with Standards like Java Verified testing and more
i) Installing or removing of programs correctly in the phone and SIM card memory
j) Synchronization of data with the calendar, phone book and programs on the computers
k) Work conditions should be stable under stress and failure recoveries
l) Localization should be correct

235: Explain Network testing.
Answer:
Another specialized field is networking. Testing in the Network is a specialized field. Good background knowledge of networking is desired. The knowledge should strongly comprise of protocols to help identify TCP or IP tuning opportunities. It is an added advantage to also know any tool of network modelling like OpNet and so on. The guidelines of operations must be determined by all the network managers, such that their users and network services find it acceptable. It is heard that network managers are challenging that the increased bandwidth will be the solution for

network issues.

There are some network characteristics that are important.

a) Levels of Utilization

b) Utilization of Application

c) Number of network users

Each network should have individual evaluation. Then, the network testing will grow up around the significant criteria for that network. The basic metrics to be confined while network testing is the output queue length, throughput, and so on. Network testing must have a finely defined and properly implemented strategy which will guide the network manager to predict network operations. Network testing is understood as the actual measurement and record of a network's operation situation over a period of time. It also involves recording the current condition of network operation, as a basis for control or comparison.

236: What factors contribute to Network operation?
Answer:
Network operations will be an important asset in troubleshooting a scenario, if the regular operating condition of the network is understood. Further, an appropriate implementation and a well defined strategy for network testing help's the network manager determine the network operations. An established-reliable network testing enables the network's capacity to support new users and new applications without any speculation.

a) What is to be tested is one of the first factors to establish. Once the network testing criteria are established, a standard format should be developed to allow easy recording of the test data. The user is enabled to develop a network specific testing table by the database tool equipped PC.

b) The next step is to create a central database. This is where reports related to all network testing and troubleshooting are kept. This serves as valuable reference information for the network. The database with more information developed, leads to easier network maintenance task. This information maintenance includes segment, user, switch, peripheral, router and bridge.

c) Once the database is developed, the network testing phase begins. The first on the list is Inventory - to set up a broad list of hardware components. One of the elementary steps in an inventory, is to record the total number of components in the network.

Now, the first step in effective network testing is established. Network testing requires engagement. It is important that network testing should not be performed after the network modifications or issues. This involves in proper development which creates a record of the network to provide an effective tool.

237: When is a Network testing performed?
Answer:
A complete testing of the network will allow a network manager to actively maintain the network. A properly implemented schedule for testing will provide a helpful insight to changes or trends in the daily operation of the network. The network manager may get this insight to predict operation for a given load or expect trouble produced by new services.

In an ideal world, network testing will be performed for each loop or segment for an extended period of time, such as a complete week. Analyzing the long period network testing results will then be determined by a testing schedule. From this primary long term test, troubles will be selected and determined. This trouble spot might have elevated levels of error conditions or have exceptionally high utilization. This should determine as to what is regular, acceptable, and undesirable for a certain network. Considering the resources and time, network testing every segment might be difficult. In this case, selecting the crucial or challenging networks for testing is ideal.

238: Explain LAN network and its testing.

Answer:

The LAN can be expanded as Local area network. It is a collection of many computers (considered as clients) connected to one major single sharing computer (known as a server) and other associated devices with a common communication line. It is the connection of a local network within a small area of geography. An example can be, within an office building with a few users. Normally, devices that are connected share the properties of a single server or processor. This server has data storage and applications that are shared commonly between multiple users of computers. A LAN may also be used in a home with just one user to two. As an example, this can be using a PC and a laptop with a wireless data card and modem in a home network. There are foremost local area network technologies such as Ethernet, Token Ring, FDDI, and ARCNET.

Testing for a LAN network is done to check its speed in a real time scenario apart from the bandwidth service provider and the computer server capacity.

The speed of networks widely varies depending on how they are constructed and being used. There are networks that run faster, more than 100 times compared to others. Knowing the speed of a network is important and can have several reasons for this.

Testing is done in several ways.

a) Downloading a large file and checking its time taken to finish downloading

b) Service provider internet connection performance is to be measured as promised

c) To check if web browser issues are slow due to network problems

d) To run 'speed test (measuring speed in a short period of time by observing time taken for a specified amount of data transfer)' varieties and examines the connection speed of a network and interpret the results. Commonly used test is 'ping' time for checking delay.

e) Checking 'data rate' on the network. It is the number of

computer bits travelled in one second over the connection. Data rates are in thousands, billions and millions of bits/second.

239: Explain WAN network and its testing.
Answer:
On the contrary, to a LAN, WAN is spread across large areas of geography (outside the office connections and home connection). WAN can be expanded as a Wide area Network. It is a network connection of servers and its clients through a secured communication line over different areas. Here, security is more crucial and needs to be ensured with various types of tests conducted. There are two kinds of testing done, external and internal testing.

During an external testing, the test team or the audit team is made as a possible impostor trying to break in through an IP address to know the details of the firewalls, subsystems, in house routers and other behind systems.

The first step is to find out the vulnerabilities in the list of applications and Internet services being offered. Here the information derived may or may not be necessary, but will at least offer information useful to the intruder. Most importantly, searching does not require extraordinary knowledge. A DNS lookup on the domain of the company can provide an address at the beginning, and then scanning can be extended to the whole network in which it is enclosed.

The next step is to commence a broad choice of automated attacks to identify the survival of any weak points that could be unnoticed without extreme effort of the intruder. These may be the factors of lack of security during design, services or hosts, network misconfiguration, or using outdated software techniques. In this testing an entire network can be plotted out from a distinct IP address with the right equipment. This data is then used to attack and negotiate the network from the outside of internal testing.

Internal testing differs from external testing; internal testing also places the tester as an intruder that successfully breaks into the WAN. This intruder once in, can get access to the resources that provide external security on the WAN at all locations.

240: Explain threats of WAN security and its measures.

Answer:

There are WAN security problems and many problems can be avoided by maintaining awareness in stages of network engineering with security in planning, designing and implementing. Other troubles can result from weak operational procedures and practice and this could be due to lack of in depth security knowledge or focus within the administration of the network.

The general areas of large threats for WAN security are below.

a) **Configuration of Systems** - A weak point is created when the system component is configured insecurely. They are, access control mechanisms - like routers password authentication have not been enabled or default configuration values are present or the systems security is violated through extensions being made.

b) **Software expiry** - A bug in a deployed program on the network can create a negative point. Prior discovery has to be made for the organization to know about this bug. The criminal software has to be disconnected or restricted from regular users. Else the other way to fix the bug is to install the latest updated security.

c) **Insecure design of network** – Improper designing of the network leads to security concerns negligence, or inadequate configuration of applications is being implemented on the network. Also, many points of access to a network may not be secured, which provides probable intruders into a network.

d) **Visibility of the Internet** -The Internet offers much information with organizations connected, like IP address allocation, technical contacts, and registrations of names. This information is harmless and is indeed necessary for the Internet functionality, but at some point there may be potential intruders offered with excessive details. Any such information of internal networks should be disclosed to the public.

241: Explain hardware testing.
Answer:
A hardware testing is performed through a common test platform - CTP. This is also known as an open test standard - OTS. It is a group of specifications with defined testing methods for various components of electronic and computer systems to be sold as a complete product. The goal is to ensure reliability in hardware and software testing procedures from the theoretical and design phases from manufacturer to distributor. Computer peripherals, PC or computer and electronic systems, often include intricate devices, programs, circuits and interfaces. They must all work together with a combination of situations and applications. An OTS can be an element of quality assurance program. This method can optimize the use of test equipment, reduce the cost of testing equipments and training, and increase production efficiency. Another suggested way of hardware testing is Stress testing. This should bring hardware of computers to inflated levels of stress, to ensure steadiness when used in a common environment. This stress can be, task type, thermal load, and extremes of workload, memory use, voltages, or clock speed. CPU and Memory are two commonly stress tested components. This method of running stress test can also identify the need of further cooling for the computer. If an over -clocked CPU or graphics card, consistently over-heats and shuts down during a stress test, it's time to leave the stock cooler, insert a few case fans, and consider liquid cooling if possible.
One way to ensure the existence of hardware trouble is by exhausting through troubleshooting all software tests. Check to ensure stability and reliability of the system. Erratic hardware can cause misery when heftier tasks are performed such as video editing or gaming.

242: Explain Hardware Diagnostic in software testing.

Answer:

Hardware diagnostic is a process of finding trouble with computer system hardware. These diagnostic systems can be executed by the user or interior programs initiated by the control system from within the hardware itself.

This diagnostic can also be a tool and is available from many service providers such as HP and more. Basic hardware diagnostics cover the essential systems in a computer on every booting; they are the chipset, the processor and the memory. These diagnostic systems often give a vital early warning of system failure or breakdown.

Hardware diagnostic systems are basically of two types of purposes, single point and multi. A single point diagnostic program will check only for a specific piece of hardware which is very specific. These Single diagnostic programs are regularly supplied by hardware manufacturers and are good beginners in identifying peculiar computer behavior.

A multipurpose diagnostic, will check several pieces for problems of hardware. Due to which, there are more chances to miss on small problems that a single purpose diagnostic catches. This type often checks items that are strange, such as a network system or the monitor.

Internal diagnostics programs usually have two locations, computer operating system or the hardware driver. They are regularly a single point diagnosis. These programs will usually run in the back of the computer whenever it is in action. An operating system's scan checks for malfunction in the answers it receives from hardware, discovering them only after the hardware actually begins to fail. The computer control system executes a hardware diagnostic, which functions on a very essential level. It normally monitors response times and power levels relative to data validity.

Driver diagnostic systems often report strange behavior in a piece of hardware when it becomes obvious with close attention. A widely held active scans take place during the booting series with single purpose programs checking on various computer systems. These are different diagnosis of hardware.

243: Explain reasons for failure of computer hardware.
Answer:
There are other ways of testing computer hardware with reasons of failures.

a) Test the hard drive of a computer for failures
A terrible hard drive can raise a collection of different problems on the computer. Importantly, there are other reasons for failure of bad disk drive.
   i) Errors when copying, reading, deleting or moving data on the computer.
   ii) OS unable to boot.
   iii) Extremely slow.
   iv) Computer re-boot or other random errors.

b) Test the memory, Motherboard and CPU and determine if it is bad
A poor memory, an awful CPU or motherboard can cause many issues on the computer. Below are a few possible issues that one may encounter.
   i) Booting does not happen instead getting a beep code on the computer.
   ii) Computer crashes randomly causing, showing error messages for general Protection, Fatal Exceptions, Illegal Operations, etc.
   iii) Random computer rebooting.
   iv) Installing Windows or other programs fail.

244: Explain embedded testing.
Answer:
The process of employing smart techniques by the trained testers intended to gauge the features and potentials of a software program is known as embedded testing. The test ensures software specified requirements. Testing the software is crucial to support

its excellence. Embedded testing is a better way to ensure major area safety, including railways, aviation, medical equipments, vehicle industry and more. To get certification of software, strict and careful testing is required. Earlier, testing the embedded software applications were tiring process and time consuming. The latest technological development has made this easier and less time involved with delivering error free results. It is also cost effective and simple. Embedded testing checks for good quality software with all the requirements covered.

The quality, excellence and superiority of software performance are essential as they are employed in all spheres of life. A minor fault can lead to obnoxious incidents and cause huge damages in the industries.

Embedded testing is designed to evaluate the tool and software testing is done identically by both developers and software testers.

245: What is designing hardware test procedure?
Answer:
Designing the test procedure to confirm that equipment works correctly throughout the life cycle should be done with the following.

    a) Inspection of equipment,
    b) Staging of the subsystem,
    c) Installation of System or network.

Inspection of Equipment
Perform tests on equipment received and ensure for no factory equipment damages or defects during transit. Tests include diagnostics, burn-in tests and physical inspections.

Staging of the Subsystem
After installation and loading of peripherals and equipment options according to the software configuration standard, staging tests should be performed to make certain that the equipment functions properly as one unit. Additional diagnostic tests are also included, to implement the installed peripherals and options.

Installation of System or Network
Installation tests should be performed at the system level to

exhibit that networking components and major processing operate as expected. For instance, procedures that test servers and client workstations using client or server applications are included. Procedures that test connectivity between network components are also included.

This page is intentionally left blank

Metrics and Measures

246: What are Software Test Metrics?

Answer:

An analysis of measurement and improvement of the software testing is known as Test Metrics. Test metrics contain essential data which provide insight of the activities such as the product under test or the testing itself. Test Metrics are followed differently among companies based on methodologies and standardization. The two types of Test metrics are Product and Process metrics.

One class of the Test Metrics that records testing activities is Test Process metrics:

    a)   The total number of Test Cases

    b)   The number of Test Cases Executed

    c)   The number of Passed Test Cases

    d)   The number of Failed Test Cases

    e)   The number of un-executed test cases

    f)   The rate of Execution

    g)   The total number of Defects Raised

    h)   The presented delivery date

Another class of Test metrics that records the bug activities is Test Product metrics:

    a)   Number of open bugs

    b)   The number of 'resolved' bugs

    c)   Number of bugs opened per day

    d)   Number of open bugs 'pass' per day

    e)   Number of open bugs 'pass' per test case

    f)   Comparing the rate of bugs resolved with the rate of bugs being opened

    g)   The number of stale bugs (older days)

247: What are the Types of Matrix used?

Answer:

The term Software metrics holds many activities, which involves some amount of measurement of software with the ultimate goal of improving quality. The three types of Matrix and they are:

QAM - Quality Assurance Matrix: To test whether quality is being achieved as expected
The activities included are:
   a) Estimation models for cost and measures of efforts
   b) Measures of productivity and quality and their respective models
   c) Collection of Data
   d) Reliability models
   e) Evaluation of performance and its models
   f) Management of Complexity and Structural metrics
   g) Assessing the maturity capability
   h) Assessment of methods and tools

TMM - Test Management Matrix: To find coverage of testing (open versus completion) and the ways of testing. The mapping between the test cases and the requirements is TMM. TMM is very helpful in the case of requirements changes.

PCM - Process Compatibility Matrix: PCM is the assessment of the testing process for a forthcoming project, depending on the current project experience. PCM involves changes that may or may not be required depending on the old project.

248: Explain Requirement Traceability Matrix.
Answer:
A requirement in a software project is the set of parameters to which the output or outcome of the system or product should confirm. Requirements management is disciplined with documentation, tracing, prioritizing, and analysis and agree on project deliverables. This requires configuration management setup and deals with modifications or alterations in hardware, documentations, software, firmware and measurement. Such alterations are in the line of changes and it is very important to note all the significant changes in stages which form the bottom line identifications. Thus, requirement traceability matrix is a document to track the correlation between bottom line changes that make up multiple relationships in order to establish its totality. The requirement traceability matrix uses basic list such as

Business or User specifications or Functional specifications. Tráceability Matrix is an instrument for validation team and for the auditors and is used to preserve the requirements to review the documentation during validation testing. This document is updated when the designing and test protocols are developed. Thus, RTM is the mapping of requirements and test cases to the specific test step.

249: What is Bidirectional Traceability?
Answer:
As per requirement traceability matrix, when requirements are mapped to test cases and the same is performed vice versa, it is called bidirectional traceability. As the very word suggests, bidirectional means both forward and backward. This is also known as Vertical and Horizontal traceability matrix.
Vertical traceability matrix is the requirements traceability across modules. Horizontal Traceability is the traceability matrix is the requirements across all the development stages like,

a) Design
b) Module
c) Unit Testing
d) Integration testing
e) Systems testing

Normally, traceability identifies the origin of items (like the needs of the customer) and tracks these items as they move through the ladder of the Breakdown Structure of work to the project teams and ultimately to the customer. 'Bidirectional traceability' is easily achieved when the requirements are managed well. This is carried out throughout the development process and ensures that all the basic requirements are implemented in the system and work products are mapped to a valid source.

HR Questions

Review these typical interview questions and think about how you would answer them. Read the answers listed; you will find best possible answers along with strategies and suggestions.

1: Tell me about a time when you worked additional hours to finish a project.
Answer:
It's important for your employer to see that you are dedicated to your work, and willing to put in extra hours when required or when a job calls for it. However, be careful when explaining why you were called to work additional hours – for instance, did you have to stay late because you set goals poorly earlier in the process? Or on a more positive note, were you working additional hours because a client requested for a deadline to be moved up on short notice? Stress your competence and willingness to give 110% every time.

2: Tell me about a time when your performance exceeded the duties and requirements of your job.
Answer:
If you're a great candidate for the position, this should be an easy question to answer – choose a time when you truly went above and beyond the call of duty, and put in additional work or voluntarily took on new responsib-ilities. Remain humble, and express gratitude for the learning opportunity, as well as confidence in your ability to give a repeat performance.

3: What is your driving attitude about work?
Answer:
There are many possible good answers to this question, and the interviewer primarily wants to see that you have a great passion for the job and that you will remain motivated in your career if hired. Some specific driving forces behind your success may include hard work, opportunity, growth potential, or success.

4: Do you take work home with you?
Answer:
It is important to first clarify that you are always willing to take work home when necessary, but you want to emphasize as well that it has not been an issue for you in the past. Highlight skills

such as time management, goal-setting, and multi-tasking, which can all ensure that work is completed at work.

5: Describe a typical work day to me.
Answer:
There are several important components in your typical work day, and an interviewer may derive meaning from any or all of them, as well as from your ability to systematically lead him or her through the day. Start at the beginning of your day and proceed chronologically, making sure to emphasize steady productivity, time for review, goal-setting, and prioritizing, as well as some additional time to account for unexpected things that may arise.

6: Tell me about a time when you went out of your way at your previous job.
Answer:
Here it is best to use a specific example of the situation that required you to go out of your way, what your specific position would have required that you did, and how you went above that. Use concrete details, and be sure to include the results, as well as reflection on what you learned in the process.

7: Are you open to receiving feedback and criticisms on your job performance, and adjusting as necessary?
Answer:
This question has a pretty clear answer – yes – but you'll need to display a knowledge as to why this is important. Receiving feedback and criticism is one thing, but the most important part of that process is to then implement it into your daily work. Keep a good attitude, and express that you always appreciate constructive feedback.

8: What inspires you?
Answer:
You may find inspiration in nature, reading success stories, or mastering a difficult task, but it's important that your inspiration

is positively-based and that you're able to listen and tune into it when it appears. Keep this answer generally based in the professional world, but where applicable, it may stretch a bit into creative exercises in your personal life that, in turn, help you in achieving career objectives.

9: How do you inspire others?
Answer:
This may be a difficult question, as it is often hard to discern the effects of inspiration in others. Instead of offering a specific example of a time when you inspired someone, focus on general principles such as leading by example that you employ in your professional life. If possible, relate this to a quality that someone who inspired you possessed, and discuss the way you have modified or modeled it in your own work.

10: How do you make decisions?
Answer:
This is a great opportunity for you to wow your interviewer with your decisiveness, confidence, and organizational skills. Make sure that you outline a process for decision-making, and that you stress the importance of weighing your options, as well as in trusting intuition. If you answer this question skillfully and with ease, your interviewer will trust in your capability as a worker.

11: What are the most difficult decisions for you to make?
Answer:
Explain your relationship to decision-making, and a general synopsis of the process you take in making choices. If there is a particular type of decision that you often struggle with, such as those that involve other people, make sure to explain why that type of decision is tough for you, and how you are currently engaged in improving your skills.

12: When making a tough decision, how do you gather information?

Answer:

If you're making a tough choice, it's best to gather information from as many sources as possible. Lead the interviewer through your process of taking information from people in different areas, starting first with advice from experts in your field, feedback from coworkers or other clients, and by looking analytically at your own past experiences.

13: Tell me about a decision you made that did not turn out well.

Answer:

Honesty and transparency are great values that your interviewer will appreciate – outline the choice you made, why you made it, the results of your poor decision – and finally (and most importantly!) what you learned from the decision. Give the interviewer reason to trust that you wouldn't make a decision like that again in the future.

14: Are you able to make decisions quickly?

Answer:

You may be able to make decisions quickly, but be sure to communicate your skill in making sound, thorough decisions as well. Discuss the importance of making a decision quickly, and how you do so, as well as the necessity for each decision to first be well-informed.

15: Ten years ago, what were your career goals?

Answer:

In reflecting back to what your career goals were ten years ago, it's important to show the ways in which you've made progress in that time. Draw distinct links between specific objectives that you've achieved, and speak candidly about how it felt to reach those goals. Remain positive, upbeat, and growth-oriented, even if you haven't yet achieved all of the goals you set out to reach.

16: Tell me about a weakness you used to have, and how you changed it.

Answer:

Choose a non-professional weakness that you used to have, and outline the process you went through in order to grow past it. Explain the weakness itself, why it was problematic, the action steps you planned, how you achieved them, and the end result.

17: Tell me about your goal-setting process.

Answer:

When describing your goal-setting process, clearly outline the way that you create an outline for yourself. It may be helpful to offer an example of a particular goal you've set in the past, and use this as a starting point to guide the way you created action steps, check-in points, and how the goal was eventually achieved.

18: Tell me about a time when you solved a problem by creating actionable steps to follow.

Answer:

This question will help the interviewer to see how you talented you are in outlining, problem resolution, and goal-setting. Explain thoroughly the procedure of outlining the problem, establishing steps to take, and then how you followed the steps (such as through check-in points along the way, or intermediary goals).

19: Where do you see yourself five years from now?

Answer:

Have some idea of where you would like to have advanced to in the position you're applying for, over the next several years. Make sure that your future plans line up with you still working for the company, and stay positive about potential advancement. Focus on future opportunities, and what you're looking forward to – but make sure your reasons for advancement are admirable, such as greater experience and the chance to learn, rather than simply being out for a higher salary.

20: When in a position, do you look for opportunities to promote?
Answer:
There's a fine balance in this question – you want to show the interviewer that you have initiative and motivation to advance in your career, but not at the expense of appearing opportunistic or selfishly-motivated. Explain that you are always open to growth opportunities, and very willing to take on new responsibilities as your career advances.

21: On a scale of 1 to 10, how successful has your life been?
Answer:
Though you may still have a long list of goals to achieve, it's important to keep this answer positively-focused. Choose a high number between 7 and 9, and explain that you feel your life has been largely successful and satisfactory as a result of several specific achievements or experiences. Don't go as high as a 10, as the interviewer may not believe your response or in your ability to reason critically.

22: What is your greatest goal in life?
Answer:
It's okay for this answer to stray a bit into your personal life, but best if you can keep it professionally-focused. While specific goals are great, if your personal goal doesn't match up exactly with one of the company's objectives, you're better off keeping your goal a little more generic and encompassing, such as "success in my career" or "leading a happy and fulfilling life." Keep your answer brief, and show a decisive nature – most importantly, make it clear that you've already thought about this question and know what you want.

23: Tell me about a time when you set a goal in your personal life and achieved it.
Answer:
The interviewer can see that you excel at setting goals in your

professional life, but he or she also wants to know that you are consistent in your life and capable of setting goals outside of the office as well. Use an example such as making a goal to eat more healthily or to drink more water, and discuss what steps you outlined to achieve your goal, the process of taking action, and the final results as well.

24: What is your greatest goal in your career?
Answer:
Have a very specific goal of something you want to achieve in your career in mind, and be sure that it's something the position clearly puts you in line to accomplish. Offer the goal as well as your plans to get there, and emphasize clear ways in which this position will be an opportunity to work toward the goal.

25: Tell me about a time when you achieved a goal.
Answer:
Start out with how you set the goal, and why you chose it. Then, take the interviewer through the process of outlining the goal, taking steps to achieve it, the outcome, and finally, how you felt after achieving it or recognition you received. The most important part of this question includes the planning and implementation of strategies, so focus most of your time on explaining these aspects. However, the preliminary decisions and end results are also important, so make sure to include them as well.

26: What areas of your work would you still like to improve in? What are your plans to do this?
Answer:
While you may not want the interviewer to focus on things you could improve on, it's important to be self-aware of your own growth opportunities. More importantly, you can impress an interviewer by having specific goals and actions outlined in order to facilitate your growth, even if your area of improvement is something as simple as increasing sales or finding new ways to create greater efficiency.

27: Tell me about your favorite book or newspaper.
Answer:
The interviewer will look at your answer to this question in order to determine your ability to analyze and review critically. Additionally, try to choose something that is on a topic related to your field or that embodies a theme important to your work, and be able to explain how it relates. Stay away from controversial subject matter, such as politics or religion.

28: If you could be rich or famous, which would you choose?
Answer:
This question speaks to your ability to think creatively, but your answer may also give great insight to your character. If you answer rich, your interviewer may interpret that you are self-confident and don't seek approval from others, and that you like to be rewarded for your work. If you choose famous, your interviewer may gather that you like to be well-known and to deal with people, and to have the platform to deliver your message to others. Either way, it's important to back up your answer with sound reasoning.

29: If you could trade places with anyone for a week, who would it be and why?
Answer:
This question is largely designed to test your ability to think on your feet, and to come up with a reasonable answer to an outside the box question. Whoever you choose, explain your answer in a logical manner, and offer specific professional reasons that led you to choose the individual.

30: What would you say if I told you that just from glancing over your resume; I can already see three spelling mistakes?
Answer:
Clearly, your resume should be absolutely spotless – and you should be confident that it is. If your interviewer tries to make you second-guess yourself here, remain calm and poised and

assert with a polite smile that you would be quite surprised as you
are positive that your resume is error-free.

31: Tell me about your worldview.
Answer:
This question is designed to offer insight into your personality, so
be aware of how the interviewer will interpret your answer.
Speak openly and directly, and try to incorporate your own job
skills into your outlook on life. For example, discuss your beliefs
on the ways that hard work and dedication can always bring
success, or in how learning new things is one of life's greatest
gifts. It's okay to expand into general life principles here, but try
to keep your thoughts related to the professional field as well.

32: What is the biggest mistake someone could make in an interview?
Answer:
The biggest mistake that could be made in an interview is to be
caught off guard! Make sure that you don't commit whatever you
answer here, and additionally be prepared for all questions.
Other common mistakes include asking too early in the hiring
process about job benefits, not having questions prepared when
the interviewer asks if you have questions, arriving late, dressing
casually or sloppily, or showing ignorance of the position.

33: If you won the $50m lottery, what would you do with the money?
Answer:
While a question such as this may seem out of place in a job
interview, it's important to display your creative thinking and
your ability to think on the spot. It's also helpful if you choose
something admirable, yet believable, to do with the money such
as donate the first seventy percent to a charitable cause, and
divide the remainder among gifts for friends, family, and of
course, yourself.

34: Is there ever a time when honesty isn't appropriate in the workplace?

Answer:

This may be a difficult question, but the only time that honesty isn't appropriate in the workplace is perhaps when you're feeling anger or another emotion that is best kept to yourself. If this is the case, explain simply that it is best to put some thoughts aside, and clarify that the process of keeping some thoughts quiet is often enough to smooth over any unsettled emotions, thus eliminating the problem.

35: If you could travel anywhere in the world, where would it be?

Answer:

This question is meant to allow you to be creative – so go ahead and stretch your thoughts to come up with a unique answer. However, be sure to keep your answer professionally-minded. For example, choose somewhere rich with culture or that would expose you to a new experience, rather than going on an expensive cruise through the Bahamas.

36: What would I find in your refrigerator right now?

Answer:

An interviewer may ask a creative question such as this in order to discern your ability to answer unexpected questions calmly, or, to try to gain some insight into your personality. For example, candidates with a refrigerator full of junk food or take-out may be more likely to be under stress or have health issues, while a candidate with a balanced refrigerator full of nutritious staples may be more likely to lead a balanced mental life, as well.

37: If you could play any sport professionally, what would it be and what aspect draws you to it?

Answer:

Even if you don't know much about professional sports, this question might be a great opportunity to highlight some of your greatest professional working skills. For example, you may choose to play professional basketball, because you admire the teamwork and coordination that goes into creating a solid play. Or, you may choose to play professional tennis, because you consider yourself to be a go-getter with a solid work ethic and great dedication to perfecting your craft. Explain your choice simply to the interviewer without elaborating on drawn-out sports metaphors, and be sure to point out specific areas or skills in which you excel.

38: Who were the presidential and vice-presidential candidates in the 2008 elections?
Answer:
This question, plain and simple, is intended as a gauge of your intelligence and awareness. If you miss this question, you may well fail the interview. Offer your response with a polite smile, because you understand that there are some individuals who probably miss this question.

39: Explain *X task* in a few short sentences as you would to a second-grader.
Answer:
An interviewer may ask you to break down a normal job task that you would complete in a manner that a child could understand, in part to test your knowledge of the task's inner workings – but in larger part, to test your ability to explain a process in simple, basic terms. While you and your coworkers may be able to converse using highly technical language, being able to simplify a process is an important skill for any employee to have.

40: If you could compare yourself to any animal, what would it be?
Answer:
Many interviewers ask this question, and it's not to determine which character traits you think you embody – instead, the interviewer wants to see that you can think outside the box, and

that you're able to reason your way through any situation. Regardless of what animal you answer, be sure that you provide a thorough reason for your choice.

41: Who is your hero?
Answer:
Your hero may be your mother or father, an old professor, someone successful in your field, or perhaps even Wonder Woman – but keep your reasoning for your choice professional, and be prepared to offer a logical train of thought. Choose someone who embodies values that are important in your chosen career field, and answer the question with a smile and sense of passion.

42: Who would play you in the movie about your life?
Answer:
As with many creative questions that challenge an interviewee to think outside the box, the answer to this question is not as important as how you answer it. Choose a professional, and relatively non-controversial actor or actress, and then be prepared to offer specific reasoning for your choice, employing important skills or traits you possess.

43: Name five people, alive or dead, that would be at your ideal dinner party.
Answer:
Smile and sound excited at the opportunity to think outside the box when asked this question, even if it seems to come from left field. Choose dynamic, inspiring individuals who you could truly learn from, and explain what each of them would have to offer to the conversation. Don't forget to include yourself, and to talk about what you would bring to the conversation as well!

44: What is customer service?
Answer:
Customer service can be many things – and the most important

consideration in this question is that you have a creative answer. Demonstrate your ability to think outside the box by offering a confident answer that goes past a basic definition, and that shows you have truly considered your own individual view of what it means to take care of your customers. The thoughtful consideration you hold for customers will speak for itself.

45: Tell me about a time when you went out of your way for a customer.
Answer:
It's important that you offer an example of a time you truly went out of your way – be careful not to confuse something that felt like a big effort on your part, with something your employer would expect you to do anyway. Offer an example of the customer's problems, what you did to solve it, and the way the customer responded after you took care of the situation.

46: How do you gain confidence from customers?
Answer:
This is a very open-ended question that allows you to show your customer service skills to the interviewer. There are many possible answers, and it is best to choose something that you've had great experience with, such as "by handling situations with transparency," "offering rewards," or "focusing on great communication." Offer specific examples of successes you've had.

47: Tell me about a time when a customer was upset or agitated – how did you handle the situation?
Answer:
Similarly to handling a dispute with another employee, the most important part to answering this question is to first set up the scenario, offer a step-by-step guide to your particular conflict resolution style, and end by describing the way the conflict was resolved. Be sure that in answering questions about your own conflict resolution style, that you emphasize the importance of open communication and understanding from both parties, as

well as a willingness to reach a compromise or other solution.

48: When can you make an exception for a customer?
Answer:
Exceptions for customers can generally be made when in accordance with company policy or when directed by a supervisor. Display an understanding of the types of situations in which an exception should be considered, such as when a customer has endured a particular hardship, had a complication with an order, or at a request.

49: What would you do in a situation where you were needed by both a customer and your boss?
Answer:
While both your customer and your boss have different needs of you and are very important to your success as a worker, it is always best to try to attend to your customer first – however, the key is explaining to your boss why you are needed urgently by the customer, and then to assure your boss that you will attend to his or her needs as soon as possible (unless it's absolutely an urgent matter).

50: What is the most important aspect of customer service?
Answer:
While many people would simply state that customer satisfaction is the most important aspect of customer service, it's important to be able to elaborate on other important techniques in customer service situations. Explain why customer service is such a key part of business, and be sure to expand on the aspect that you deem to be the most important in a way that is reasoned and well-thought out.

51: Is it best to create low or high expectations for a customer?
Answer:
You may answer this question either way (after, of course, determining that the company does not have a clear opinion on

the matter). However, no matter which way you answer the question, you must display a thorough thought process, and very clear reasoning for the option you chose. Offer pros and cons of each, and include the ultimate point that tips the scale in favor of your chosen answer.

INDEX

Software Testing Interview Questions

SDLC and STLC

1. What is Software and why is it necessary?
2. Explain Software development life cycle (SDLC) and its phases.
3. What kinds of businesses use software and how?
4. What is STLC and how is it related to SDLC?
5. With a specific process, how do you differentiate STLC from SDLC?
6. Who is involved in an SDLC and STLC?
7. What is a project life cycle?
8. Provide details of project life cycle phases.
9. What is the difference between QA and QC and Quality management?
10. Why is quality important and who is looking for quality?
11. What is meaning of prototype in SDLC?
12. What is the difference between project, product, and application?
13. What are the objectives of a good software testing?
14. What is the goal of a tester and how to attain it?
15. What is the cause of software failure?

Testing and Methods of Testing

16. What is Testing or Software testing?
17. What is Test Control?
18. What is Test Estimation and how is it done?
19. What are the different types of Test Estimation?
20. What is the difference between a Developer and a Tester?
21. What are Testing methods? Describe their characteristics.
22. What is a White box testing stage?
23. What is a Black box testing stage?
24. What is a Grey box testing?
25. What is a requirement testing?
26. What are reviews, inspections, peer review or walkthroughs?
27. What are the techniques used in white box testing?
28. Does testing start early in SDLC?
29. Do requirements change continuously and how is it done?
30. Does the software have a risk based testing, how is it resolved?
31. Define Data flow analysis testing technique.

Levels of Testing

32. What is the Myth in testing?
33. Can a Fresher without knowledge, perform manual software testing? How?
34. What are levels of testing and their use?
35. Elaborate on types of Integration testing.
36. What are the advantages of unit testing?
37. What are different types of system testing?
38. How is system testing carried out?
39. List out differences between Unit and Integration Testing.
40. What is debugging?
41. How can mistakes be classified in testing?

Types of Testing

42. What are the different types of testing?
43. What is positive and negative testing?
44. What testing types do you carry out for a constrained deadline and why?
45. What is boundary value analysis?
46. What is an equivalence class partitioning?
47. What is globalization testing?
48. What is alpha and beta stage testing?
49. Is there any difference between retesting and regression?
50. What is a checklist? How is it part of Quality?
51. Write checklist for script execution.
52. Write the checklist for defects logging.
53. What is blocking and unblocking of scripts? Provide its checklist.
54. How is a Test case executed?
55. How to perform Exploratory or Adhoc testing?
56. What is Functional testing and Non-functional testing?
57. What is Performance testing and how is it useful?
58. What is Monkey testing?
59. Explain Installation testing, Sanity and Smoke testing.
60. Explain Stress, Volume and Load testing.
61. Explain Usability and Mutation testing.
62. Explain Array testing and API testing.
63. Explain Cosmetic and Syntax testing.
64. What are Localization testing and Isolation testing?
65. What is Soak testing and Fuzz testing?
66. What is End to End testing and Compatibility testing?

67. Explain Reliability, Recovery and Security testing.
68. What are Gorilla testing and Scalability testing?
69. What are GUI testing and Spike testing?
70. Give examples for load and spike testing.
71. What is Encryption, Authentication and Authorization in testing?
72. How is Benchmark testing done?
73. Give examples of stress testing.
74. Explain the state of UAT testing.
75. Define the term 'Vulnerability' and its use in testing.
76. Explain Testing Limitations.
77. Explain Test Monitoring.
78. Give an example of Integration Testing.
79. What are Component testing and Configuration testing?
80. Give an example of real case testing scenario for Work flow testing.
81. Give a real case testing scenario for Functional testing.
82. What is a Cookie and why is it used?
83. How is a Cookie setting carried out?
84. What test cases are written for a Cookie setting?
85. When is a Parallel live testing stage used?
86. Elaborate on Game testing and its importance
87. What is Cloud testing?
88. What are examples of security testing?
89. What are Binary testing and Branch testing?
90. What are Breadth testing and Code driven testing?
91. What is Benchmark testing?
92. Explain Cross browser testing and how is it different from compatibility testing.
93. Explain the meaning of Simulation and its relation with computer testing.
94. Describe Pilot testing.
95. Describe Penetration testing.
96. Describe Documentation testing, Ramp testing and Scripted testing.
97. What are Comparison testing and Pair testing?
98. Explain Passive testing and Data driven testing.
99. How is database testing done?
100. What is a Usecase? What is the attribute of Usecase?
101. Explain an Emulator.
102. Explain testing in web application architecture.
103. Explain VSS.
104. What is backend testing using SQL?

105. What is Model based testing approach?
106. What is Migration testing?
107. Explain Migration testing approaches in detail.
108. How is portlet testing done?

Testing Models or Process

109. What are different SDLC models and how is it necessary?
110. Explain Waterfall model and its use in SDLC.
111. What are the advantages and disadvantages of Waterfall model?
112. What is Incremental model in SDLC?
113. Explain advantages and disadvantages of Incremental model.
114. Explain Agile model and its usage today. How is it advantageous?
115. What is V model in SDLC?
116. Explain the V model with a graphical representation.
117. What are advantages and disadvantages in V Model?
118. Explain Test Driven (TDD) Model approach.
119. Explain Test Driven (TDD) Model advantages and disadvantages.
120. Explain RAD approach.
121. What are the advantages and disadvantages in RAD approach?
122. Explain Spiral Model approach in SDLC.
123. List the advantages and disadvantages of the Spiral model.
124. Explain the RUP model approach in SDLC.
125. Explain RUP model advantages and disadvantages.
126. Explain COTS model approach for software development.
127. Where is COTS used?
128. Explain advantages and disadvantages in a COTS Model.
129. Explain FDD model in SDLC.
130. Explain advantages and disadvantages of the FDD model approach.
131. What is Scrum Model in SDLC?
132. Explain advantages and disadvantages of Scrum model.
133. What is XP Model approach in SDLC?
134. Explain XP Model process in detail.
135. Explain advantages and disadvantages of the XP Model process.
136. What is DSDM Model in SDLC?
137. Explain advantages and disadvantages of DSDM Model.
138. What is DDD Model in SDLC?
139. Explain advantages and disadvantages of DDD Model.
140. How to select a Model for a process?

Testing Domains

141. What is a Desktop application testing?
142. What is a Client server application and its testing?
143. What is a Web application testing?
144. Explain detailed Web application testing.
145. What is the difference between the Web application testing and Client Server testing?
146. What are Domains in testing?
147. What skills are required for Domain testing?
148. What if you don't have enough domain knowledge?
149. Explain BFSI domain testing.
150. Explain Search Engine domain testing.
151. Explain Healthcare domain testing.
152. Explain Retail domain testing.
153. Explain E-commerce domain testing.
154. Explain Telecom domain testing.
155. Explain Wireless application testing.
156. What is mobile application testing and strategies?
157. What are the challenges involved in Mobile web application testing?
158. Explain Protocol testing.
159. Explain Protocol conformance testing.
160. What is VoIP application testing?
161. Explain testing method for VoIP applications.
162. Explain Cloud computing and its testing.

Testing Tools

163. Mention different tools in testing.
164. Explain about the Load testing tool.
165. Explain the functionality of JIRA tool.
166. What are the requirements of JIRA?
167. Explain the functionality of Bugzilla tool.
168. Explain the features of Bugzilla tool.
169. How does the Bugzilla tool function?
170. Explain the functionality of SoapUI.
171. What is a Configuration management tool?
172. What is TestLink?

Project Management in Testing

173. What is a code coverage tool?

174. What can be the general causes of bugs in software?
175. What are technical types of bugs?
176. What are types of faults?
177. What is a segmentation fault?
178. How is testing done in Software Project management?
179. Explain Test strategy in detail.
180. Explain a bug life cycle.
181. What is a bug management?
182. How to achieve good test cases or what are the thumb rules to write good test cases?
183. What is the Scope of testing?
184. What are the 'Defect Density' and its uses?
185. What are a Defect Management system and its features?
186. What is Test Coverage?
187. What is a Test Case Design?
188. What is the term 'release', 'build' and 'version' in software testing?
189. Explain Priority and its types.
190. Explain Severity and its types.
191. Give an example of a high severity and low priority.
192. Give an example of a high severity and high priority.
193. Give an example of a low severity and high priority.
194. Give an example of a low severity and low priority.
195. Explain a Test Scenario.
196. Explain the Test Scenario and Test case with an example.
197. What are the Test Deliverables?
198. What is the difference between Testing method and Testing Methodology?
199. What is a Test Suite?
200. What is a test report and content of test report?
201. What is a high level and low level test case?
202. What is the database testing?
203. How to write and document a Test case?
204. What are the different Testing environments?
205. What are the types of Design Documentation?
206. Write test cases for functional testing for the website page 'Google.com'.

Testing Industries

207. What is Automation in testing and how did it evolve?
208. What are the major Automated Industry Standard Testing

Frameworks?
209. Why testing is needed in the financial industry?
210. What is outsourced testing in the industry?
211. What is on-site and offshore testing?
212. What are the On-site and Offshore testing responsibilities?
213. What is e-commerce testing?
214. What are the features for testing e-commerce site?

Standards of Testing
215. What are the standards of software testing?
216. Explain about an Audit.
217. What is Process Audit?
218. What is Product Audit?
219. What are the advantages of Product Audit in an industry?
220. What is SPC?
221. What is the basic ISO testing standard?
222. Explain Quality System.
223. Explain Total Quality Management.
224. Explain Quality Policy.
225. Explain Quality Circle.
226. Explain Quality Audit in Software Industry.
227. What is an IEEE testing standard?
228. Mention different IEEE testing standards.
229. What is ANSI, CMMI and SEI testing standards?
230. What are the levels of CMM/CMMI standard?

Devices Testing
231. What are types of mobile application testing?
232. Why is Mobile application testing done?
233. How do mobile technologies affect testing?
234. Explain the features for testing mobile application.
235. Explain Network testing.
236. What factors contribute to Network operation?
237. When is a Network testing performed?
238. Explain LAN network and its testing.
239. Explain WAN network and its testing.
240. Explain threats of WAN security and its measures.
241. Explain hardware testing.
242. Explain Hardware Diagnostic in software testing.
243. Explain reasons for failure of computer hardware.

244. Explain embedded testing.
245. What is designing hardware test procedure?

Metrics and Measures

246. What are Software Test Metrics?
247. What are the Types of Matrix used?
248. Explain Requirement Traceability Matrix.
249. What is Bidirectional Traceability?

HR Questions

1: Tell me about a time when you worked additional hours to finish a project.

2: Tell me about a time when your performance exceeded the duties and requirements of your job.

3: What is your driving attitude about work?

4: Do you take work home with you?

5: Describe a typical work day to me.

6: Tell me about a time when you went out of your way at your previous job.

7: Are you open to receiving feedback and criticisms on your job performance, and adjusting as necessary?

8: What inspires you?

9: How do you inspire others?

10: How do you make decisions?

11: What are the most difficult decisions for you to make?

12: When making a tough decision, how do you gather information?

13: Tell me about a decision you made that did not turn out well.

14: Are you able to make decisions quickly?

15: Ten years ago, what were your career goals?

16: Tell me about a weakness you used to have, and how you changed it.

17: Tell me about your goal-setting process.

18: Tell me about a time when you solved a problem by creating actionable steps to follow.

19: Where do you see yourself five years from now?

20: When in a position, do you look for opportunities to promote?

21: On a scale of 1 to 10, how successful has your life been?

22: What is your greatest goal in life?

23: Tell me about a time when you set a goal in your personal life and achieved it.

24: What is your greatest goal in your career?

25: Tell me about a time when you achieved a goal.

26: What areas of your work would you still like to improve in? What are your plans to do this?

27: Tell me about your favorite book or newspaper.

28: If you could be rich or famous, which would you choose?

29: If you could trade places with anyone for a week, who would it be and why?

30: What would you say if I told you that just from glancing over your resume, I can already see three spelling mistakes?

31: Tell me about your worldview.

32: What is the biggest mistake someone could make in an interview?

33: If you won the $50m lottery, what would you do with the money?

34: Is there ever a time when honesty isn't appropriate in the workplace?

35: If you could travel anywhere in the world, where would it be?

36: What would I find in your refrigerator right now?

37: If you could play any sport professionally, what would it be and what aspect draws you to it?

38: Who were the presidential and vice-presidential candidates in the 2008 elections?

39: Explain X *task* in a few short sentences as you would to a second-grader.

40: If you could compare yourself to any animal, what would it be?

41: Who is your hero?

42: Who would play you in the movie about your life?

43: Name five people, alive or dead, that would be at your ideal dinner party.

44: What is customer service?

45: Tell me about a time when you went out of your way for a customer.

46: How do you gain confidence from customers?

47: Tell me about a time when a customer was upset or agitated – how did you handle the situation?

48: When can you make an exception for a customer?

49: What would you do in a situation where you were needed by both a customer and your boss?

50: What is the most important aspect of customer service?

51: Is it best to create low or high expectations for a customer?

Some of the following titles might also be handy:

1. .NET Interview Questions You'll Most Likely Be Asked
2. 200 Interview Questions You'll Most Likely Be Asked
3. Access VBA Programming Interview Questions You'll Most Likely Be Asked
4. Adobe ColdFusion Interview Questions You'll Most Likely Be Asked
5. Advanced Excel Interview Questions You'll Most Likely Be Asked
6. Advanced JAVA Interview Questions You'll Most Likely Be Asked
7. Advanced SAS Interview Questions You'll Most Likely Be Asked
8. AJAX Interview Questions You'll Most Likely Be Asked
9. Algorithms Interview Questions You'll Most Likely Be Asked
10. Android Development Interview Questions You'll Most Likely Be Asked
11. Ant & Maven Interview Questions You'll Most Likely Be Asked
12. Apache Web Server Interview Questions You'll Most Likely Be Asked
13. Artificial Intelligence Interview Questions You'll Most Likely Be Asked
14. ASP.NET Interview Questions You'll Most Likely Be Asked
15. Automated Software Testing Interview Questions You'll Most Likely Be Asked
16. Base SAS Interview Questions You'll Most Likely Be Asked
17. BEA WebLogic Server Interview Questions You'll Most Likely Be Asked
18. C & C++ Interview Questions You'll Most Likely Be Asked
19. C# Interview Questions You'll Most Likely Be Asked
20. C++ Internals Interview Questions You'll Most Likely Be Asked
21. CCNA Interview Questions You'll Most Likely Be Asked
22. Cloud Computing Interview Questions You'll Most Likely Be Asked
23. Computer Architecture Interview Questions You'll Most Likely Be Asked
24. Computer Networks Interview Questions You'll Most Likely Be Asked
25. Core JAVA Interview Questions You'll Most Likely Be Asked
26. Data Structures & Algorithms Interview Questions You'll Most Likely Be Asked
27. Data WareHousing Interview Questions You'll Most Likely Be Asked
28. EJB 3.0 Interview Questions You'll Most Likely Be Asked
29. Entity Framework Interview Questions You'll Most Likely Be Asked
30. Fedora & RHEL Interview Questions You'll Most Likely Be Asked
31. GNU Development Interview Questions You'll Most Likely Be Asked
32. Hibernate, Spring & Struts Interview Questions You'll Most Likely Be Asked
33. HTML, XHTML and CSS Interview Questions You'll Most Likely Be Asked
34. HTML5 Interview Questions You'll Most Likely Be Asked
35. IBM WebSphere Application Server Interview Questions You'll Most Likely Be Asked
36. iOS SDK Interview Questions You'll Most Likely Be Asked
37. Java / J2EE Design Patterns Interview Questions You'll Most Likely Be Asked
38. Java / J2EE Interview Questions You'll Most Likely Be Asked
39. Java Messaging Service Interview Questions You'll Most Likely Be Asked
40. JavaScript Interview Questions You'll Most Likely Be Asked
41. JavaServer Faces Interview Questions You'll Most Likely Be Asked
42. JDBC Interview Questions You'll Most Likely Be Asked
43. jQuery Interview Questions You'll Most Likely Be Asked
44. JSP-Servlet Interview Questions You'll Most Likely Be Asked
45. JUnit Interview Questions You'll Most Likely Be Asked
46. Linux Commands Interview Questions You'll Most Likely Be Asked
47. Linux Interview Questions You'll Most Likely Be Asked
48. Linux System Administrator Interview Questions You'll Most Likely Be Asked
49. Mac OS X Lion Interview Questions You'll Most Likely Be Asked
50. Mac OS X Snow Leopard Interview Questions You'll Most Likely Be Asked
51. Microsoft Access Interview Questions You'll Most Likely Be Asked

52. Microsoft Excel Interview Questions You'll Most Likely Be Asked
53. Microsoft Powerpoint Interview Questions You'll Most Likely Be Asked
54. Microsoft Word Interview Questions You'll Most Likely Be Asked
55. MySQL Interview Questions You'll Most Likely Be Asked
56. NetSuite Interview Questions You'll Most Likely Be Asked
57. Networking Interview Questions You'll Most Likely Be Asked
58. OOPS Interview Questions You'll Most Likely Be Asked
59. Operating Systems Interview Questions You'll Most Likely Be Asked
60. Oracle DBA Interview Questions You'll Most Likely Be Asked
61. Oracle E-Business Suite Interview Questions You'll Most Likely Be Asked
62. ORACLE PL/SQL Interview Questions You'll Most Likely Be Asked
63. Perl Programming Interview Questions You'll Most Likely Be Asked
64. PHP Interview Questions You'll Most Likely Be Asked
65. PMP Interview Questions You'll Most Likely Be Asked
66. Python Interview Questions You'll Most Likely Be Asked
67. RESTful JAVA Web Services Interview Questions You'll Most Likely Be Asked
68. Ruby Interview Questions You'll Most Likely Be Asked
69. Ruby on Rails Interview Questions You'll Most Likely Be Asked
70. SAP ABAP Interview Questions You'll Most Likely Be Asked
71. SAP HANA Interview Questions You'll Most Likely Be Asked
72. SAS Programming Guidelines Interview Questions You'll Most Likely Be Asked
73. Selenium Testing Tools Interview Questions You'll Most Likely Be Asked
74. Silverlight Interview Questions You'll Most Likely Be Asked
75. Software Repositories Interview Questions You'll Most Likely Be Asked
76. Software Testing Interview Questions You'll Most Likely Be Asked
77. SQL Server Interview Questions You'll Most Likely Be Asked
78. Tomcat Interview Questions You'll Most Likely Be Asked
79. UML Interview Questions You'll Most Likely Be Asked
80. Unix Interview Questions You'll Most Likely Be Asked
81. UNIX Shell Programming Interview Questions You'll Most Likely Be Asked
82. VB.NET Interview Questions You'll Most Likely Be Asked
83. Windows Server 2008 R2 Interview Questions You'll Most Likely Be Asked
84. XLXP, XSLT, XPATH, XFORMS & XQuery Interview Qu estions You'll Most Likely Be Asked
85. XML Interview Questions You'll Most Likely Be Asked

For complete list visit
www.vibrantpublishers.com

www.ingramcontent.com/pod-product-compliance
Lightning Source LLC
Chambersburg PA
CBHW070940050326
40689CB00014B/3280